Havana Living Today

Havana Living Today

Cuban Home Style Now

———

HERMES MALLEA

PRINCIPAL PHOTOGRAPHY BY **ADRIÁN FERNÁNDEZ**

RIZZOLI
NEW YORK

New York · Paris · London · Milan

Contents

Introduction

Havana is full of surprises—even for those who believe they know the city well. Following several years spent documenting the city's landmark historic homes for my book *Great Houses of Havana*, I was stunned to discover that the gracious family life associated with the city's grand houses had not disappeared with the Cuban Revolution, as was usually believed.

Beginning in 2011, I encountered stylish Havana houses brimming with personality, ones that had been created despite the island's economic hardships and isolation. Dozens of homeowners—art collectors, expats, lawyers, painters, businessmen, fashion designers, musicians, schoolteachers—welcomed me into homes that lovingly reflected their unique styles.

This book celebrates the homeowners' individual flair and ingenuity and brings the reader inside a world that has never been presented in this depth. This is the untold story of Cuba's 1 percent—in contrast to the often-told hardships faced by 99 percent of the island's citizens struggling with over-crowding, scarcities, political isolation, and financial insecurity.

International readers are familiar with the artful images of urban poverty and romantically decayed historic houses that appear to be synonymous with Havana.

Neither they, nor the majority of Havana residents have any idea that the city's elite lives in this kind of style and comfort today. It is useful to keep that reality in mind, when admiring the aesthetic personality of the houses featured in this book.

I had always assumed that the expression of individualism that had been frowned upon by the Revolution had also extended to the decoration of the Cuban home. Yet, again and again I encountered very personal homes that were—in essence—portraits of the owners who created them. Presented together, these houses tell the story of Havana at a special moment in time, when the past—still visible in a handful of "time capsule" interiors that have not yet vanished—coexists with the hopefulness of a vibrant Havana home style of the future. This book portrays the end of a world that has existed in isolation for fifty years and predicts the visual language of healthier times to come.

For generations, Havana's top architectural firms made the city beautiful, building houses in every significant architectural style of the twentieth century—from Beaux-Arts classicism and Art Deco to eclectic revivals and International Style modernism. Beginning in the early twentieth century, Havana's upper-class neighborhoods expanded westward from the original walled city as the elite occupied one progressively more exclusive community after another, leaving behind the chaos of the urban center. In my research, I came to understand the unique personality of each of these communities. The elegance of turn-of-the-century Paseo del Prado, the generous gardens and eclectic mansions of the Vedado recalling the heady Sugar Boom of the 1910s and 1920s; oceanfront Miramar with its mid-century family compounds; and Havana's most elegant neighborhood, the Country Club, where millionaires enjoyed virtual isolation. Havana's landscaped avenues, planned neighborhoods, and waterfront drives are today preserved—though down-at-heel—as are the social clubs, private schools, and fashionable churches that had formed the framework for the daily lives of upper- and middle-class families. Viewed with the city's houses, these neighborhoods and their landmark public buildings provide an idea of the sophistication of life in Havana that was interrupted by the 1959 revolution.

Following Fidel Castro's takeover, foreign companies had their assets seized. Then the businesses, land, and real estate owned by Cubans were also taken and their bank accounts frozen. During the first years of the Revolution, much of Havana's elite left the island,

assuming they would be returning when things went back to normal. A number of these homeowners left family members or servants in charge of their houses, hoping to avoid their seizure by the state. Many readers will be unable to look at these images of today's stylish houses without reliving the pain of having their own Havana homes taken by the Revolution when they chose to leave the island. There will be audiences who cannot get past the idea of departing one's country in exile, leaving behind the family home and its personal contents, inventoried and sealed for confiscation. In preparing this book I was not ignorant of these controversies.

Nor was I immune to the emotions associated with the loss of the family home. When the last of my relatives left behind our family home in Gibara, Cuba, the local government repurposed the sprawling colonial house as the town's only guesthouse. Repeated hurricane damage compounded by decades of neglect led to the recent demolition of the house where every generation of my mother's family since my great-great-grandmother had been born. The destruction of the emotional core of our clan seems all the more painful for having occurred in the past year.

The concept of the home as a refuge where it is safe to be yourself is at the core of this book. As such, the loss of that haven—as a consequence of a political situation—was a heartbreaking experience made even

PREVIOUS PAGE

Havana's modernist landmark, the Richard Neutra–designed von Schulthess house with landscape by Roberto Burle Marx, is now beautifully restored and maintained as the Swiss Ambassador's Residence.

worse by the families torn apart by ideology and exile. That antagonism between Cubans is reflected in the fear felt by Havana homeowners today—people who have lived in houses for decades, having bought or inherited these properties legally, and who dread being ousted should an heir of the original homeowner return.

With the Revolution, the construction of single-family houses in Cuba essentially ceased, as the state focused on providing housing for the masses. This was an idealistic time when design was employed to cure the country's social ills, and architecture focused on efficient construction, standardization, and the meeting of production goals. Both the elite who had up to then commissioned the creation of private residences and most of the architects who had designed them were part of that early emigration. While no new single-family houses were constructed from "the ground up" after the Revolution, the creation of personalized homes did not disappear. For the last fifty years Havana's houses have evolved in a very individual way, neither following aesthetic trends nor fashioned by design professionals. Their authentic Cuban style has been accomplished while struggling with limited resources—a testament to the famous Cuban ingenuity.

Completing this book coincided with a series of historic moments including the visit of President Barack Obama and his family to Havana, as well as the staging of international cultural events like the Rolling Stones concert and the Chanel runway show. The thaw in diplomatic relations with the United States and the increase in American tourism bring hope that a new phase in Cuba's history lies ahead. Recent Cuban reforms permitting some private enterprise are energizing areas of the city as owners renovate, launch new businesses, and create new jobs for members of the surrounding community.

Savvy designers are envisioning Havana of the future as a dynamic fusion of the city's rich architectural patrimony with what is both new and authentically Cuban. Havana's aesthetic narrative needs to be told by the Cubans themselves—yet, outsiders caution the city's designers to keep in the mind the unmistakable sense of place of the city's restored historic core and to celebrate the genuine Cuban identity found in homes like those pictured in this book. When I look at Havana through the eyes of the people who created these beautiful houses, when I hear the city's designers describe their dreams for the city they love so deeply, it is impossible not to get caught up in their optimism about the island's future.

RIGHT
In the waterfront living room of film star Jorge "Pichi" Perugorría, an iconic poster from the 1960s is hung above painted cubes created by Pichi.

1

The Revolution and the Family Home

Readers may be surprised to learn that many middle class and Old Guard families remained in their Havana homes after the 1959 revolution, living in the houses their families had inhabited for generations.

These homes provided a sense of the continuity of family life amid the political and social upheavals, which many did their best to disregard. Most of the elite families who remained were not particularly political, although some had stayed in Havana in order to make their contribution to the reshaping of Cuban society.

In many cases, the homes of this Old Guard became Treasure Caves of Family Memories, filled with cherished objects often added to by relatives and friends who went into exile. Those left behind became the custodians of the culture's legacy, the keepers of the family narrative. At the same time, ownership of a home became the family's most important financial asset.

Repurposing the use of the family home was done officially by the state, with homes made to serve a variety of uses. Mansions became cultural institutions, offices, museums, or diplomatic residences—all in service of the needs of the state. At different times, the Cuban government has authorized various forms of private enterprise in the family home, including the creation of small restaurants and rooms to rent— modest businesses where the entire family is involved. This has lead to re-imagining of the use of the home by its residents. Havana's Pre-Revolution houses of the twentieth century were built in a variety of architectural styles, including Beaux-Arts Classical, Mediterranean and Spanish Colonial Revival, Sugar Boom eclectic, Art Deco, and International Style Modernism. Each of these aesthetics connects to a different moment in the city's past, telling the story of the politics, the economy, the music, and the culture that came together in the sophisticated lifestyle of the elite who built and occupied these houses.

The Home as the Link to Old-Guard Traditions
Fichú Menocal

Feliciana "Fichú" Menocal's family home was built in the late nineteenth century for members of a clan who have lived on the island almost five hundred years. Today, the house is lived in as it always has been—with different generations of Fichú's extended family spread throughout the property. While most of her children now live abroad, they all remain connected to the island, periodically returning, responding to the particular pull of their historic family home.

Fichú's courtyard house recalls the early twentieth century, when the surrounding Vedado neighborhood sprang up to incorporate older houses like hers, which had been constructed as summer getaways from the heat of Old Havana. The house overlooks the Parque Villalón, named after Fichú's grandfather, a former minister of housing. This house—and this family—are living connections to Cuba's historic past, boasting a president of the Republic within their ranks, as well as renowned architects, politicians, and attorneys.

Fichú's house is an important protagonist in her family's story. At the time of the Revolution, she and her engineer husband, Luis Morales, lived with their children in a family-owned apartment building connected to the garden at the rear of this colonial house. Several of Fichú's siblings also lived in this building with their spouses and offspring, with Fichú's mother remaining in the main house. While most of her social class left the island following the Revolution, Fichú and her family stayed to be with Fichú's mother, who remained seemingly unaffected by the political upheavals all around her. Fichú's artist daughter, Virginia, recalls the elaborate Sunday lunches at her great-grandfather Morales's house, where both the Catholic cardinal and her great-uncle, the famed architect Leonardo Morales, were always in attendance.

Today, Fichú shares the house with Virginia and her daughters. Cuban colonial furniture and family portraits mix comfortably with Virginia's contemporary mixed-media tapestries and small sculptures. Throughout the house are Fichú's charming watercolors of butterflies and hummingbirds entwined with intricate tropical flowers—these bring in the colors and breezes of the plant-filled courtyard, an outdoor sitting room, at the center of the house.

PREVIOUS PAGE

The original parlor boasts traditional elements:
a Spanish tile wainscot and floors, "Baccarat" chandeliers, and the Cuban-made Rococo Revival furniture that
has been in the house for generations.

OPPOSITE

The rear parlor is Virginia's realm, displaying her
embroidered and encrusted artwork that complements
the colorful fan lights, or *medio-puntos*, and the striking
marble floors of the historic house.

BELOW

The simple construction and plant-filled central
courtyard attest to the origins of the house as an
informal summer getaway.

Newlyweds in a Mid-Century Landmark
Lan Gómez & Fofi Fernández

"Lan" Gómez and her late husband, Rodolfo "Fofi" Fernández, have been connected to this apartment since the days of their courtship in the late 1950s. Fofi was the architect in charge of construction for the building's designer, Mario Romañach. It took scrimping and saving, but they bought the unit just as it was completed, one year before the Revolution. While many of Cuba's Pre-Revolution architects went into exile, Fofi remained and continued working for the state. Lan, who had attended boarding school in Kentucky, taught English at the high school level. A 1970s painting by their friend the Pop artist Raúl Martínez depicts the couple and the three children whom they brought up in this home.

The apartment's spaces flow into each other through a series of interlocking volumes that make everything seem bigger. Light and air enter the apartment through louvered doors, clay tile grids, ironwork at the windows, and wood lattice transoms. The building's balconies are especially inviting because they face the relatively secluded side of the property and are enclosed with architectural screens that make them even more private and, thus, an integral part of the interior.

Lan's apartment is an introduction to the constants encountered throughout Havana's stylish homes today: bentwood furniture, mid-century modernist pieces, contemporary art, and the Tiffany-style hanging lamps that became popular in the 1970s. Paintings by friends like Raúl Martínez and Servando Cabrera Moreno, as well as Cuban art ceramics by Amelia Peláez, are the collectibles of Havana's intellectual class. The balcony displays a colorful collection of objects associated with the Afro-Cuban syncretic cults—pieces that Lan and Fofi collected for their aesthetic value. More than fifty years after the Revolution, the apartment represents the continuity of family life in spite of political upheavals—a signature of the family home in Havana.

In the front hall, a bentwood rocking chair and console table bear witness to the many European imports that have been staples of Havana's eclectic interiors.

———

BELOW
The clay-tile latticework of the generous balcony helps to ventilate the nearby kitchen while framing views of both the interior spaces and the landscape beyond.

BELOW
A collection of painted ceramic bottles and vessels by
Amelia Peláez is arranged near a plate by Jorge Fuster.

———

NEXT PAGE
Above the kitchen's pass-through is a portrait of the
family by their friend Raúl Martínez, who also painted
the bold Pop Art painting to the right.

The Family Home Officially Repurposed
El Museo Napoleonico

As Havana's mansions were expropriated by the Revolution, the city's grandest houses were given new identities and repurposed as cultural, community, and educational facilities, state-run enterprises, or multi-family housing. Thus a spectacular Art Deco villa was converted into the Cuban Institute for Friendship with the Peoples, the formal salons of a sprawling Mediterranean mansion served as a textile distribution center, and a French château within extensive gardens became the weekend gathering place for the Union of Rebel Pioneers, the socialist version of the Boy Scouts. Several of Havana's most extraordinary houses became museums, telling the stories of important historical figures or presenting art collections assembled by the very millionaires against whom the Revolution had just been waged.

Important among these is Havana's Museo Napoleonico, a Florentine Renaissance–style tower house created in 1927 for wealthy politician Orestes Ferrara by architects Evelio Govantes and Felix Cabarrocas. The fortress-like mansion is protected from its surroundings by a rusticated perimeter wall and overlooks the monumental steps that lead up to the University of Havana acropolis. In 1961, the house was seized by the Revolution and rehabilitated to display the collection of Napoleonic memorabilia assembled by sugar king Julio Lobo. Reputed to be the most comprehensive collection of its kind outside of France, these works had formerly been housed in Lobo's own Vedado mansion, which had itself been repurposed as the Revolution's Ministry of Culture.

While the Revolution's repurposing has brought new life to existing buildings, installing one millionaire's collection in the mansion of another has led to a certain blurring of narratives, with history being unwittingly rewritten. What is very clear is the pride Cubans feel both in Havana's rich architectural patrimony and in this unique collection that illustrates the sophistication of a handful of collectors at the time of the Revolution.

PREVIOUS PAGE
The double-height salon with its appropriately scaled
windows, beamed ceilings, and balconies displays some
of the furniture, military uniforms, and paintings that
form the collection.

BELOW
The beautiful dining room with its pale green upholstery
and painted architectural woodwork is a perfect setting
for Julio Lobo's collection of Napoleonic furniture and
porcelains, which are displayed as if in a home setting.

———

OPPOSITE
The interior of the house is beautifully connected to
the garden through a variety of arcades, porches, and
loggias.

The Professional Home
Alexis López & Hostal Porteria

Following the Revolution, the home became a Cuban family's most important asset. While most forms of private enterprise had been outlawed by the state, a handful of freelance businesses were permitted during the economic crisis of the 1990s, when homeowners began repurposing their houses as small restaurants or bed-and-breakfasts. More recently, additional forms of entrepreneurship have been authorized, with party spaces, furniture and clothing shops, hairdressers, and video theaters set up in the family home. A visit to many of these businesses can connect today's working-class clients to a Pre-Revolution elegance that is still palpable in these repurposed homes. Here too, foreign visitors are introduced to some of the constants of today's Havana home décor: antique wicker and bentwood pieces, mid-century modern furniture, crystal chandeliers, and contemporary Cuban art.

Alexis López has lived his entire life within the same four blocks of the Vedado, growing up in his grandparents' house surrounded by their collection of books and modern Cuban paintings. Today his home is an important stop on the Havana antiques circuit that savvy locals visit continuously. From the street, his contemporary-style house looks as if it belongs in an affluent Miami suburb. Alexis has repurposed his large home to also serve as a bed-and-breakfast, receiving tourists seeking a personalized Havana experience long before Airbnb made these home stays available to Americans. Sleeping in his eclectic guest rooms or lounging on the shaded courtyard's antique wicker seating, guests savor the intimacy of the residential Vedado neighborhood. Throughout the house Alexis displays his contemporary Cuban paintings, antique furniture, and decorations—connecting foreign visitors to the best of Cuban style with his mix of colonial and mid-century pieces. Alexis has managed to define his own personal space in the house he loves so deeply, showcasing his individual style and generous hospitality for the guests and shoppers who have become part of the home's daily life.

PREVIOUS PAGE
In the courtyard, traditional elements like the painted wicker seating and antique marble sculpture and bench are juxtaposed with a contemporary Cuban painting—summing up the owner's eclectic approach to the décor.

OPPOSITE
Neoclassical-style mahogany rockers are the signature of the traditional Cuban front parlor, a room here lit by banks of modern arched windows.

———

BELOW
The double-height courtyard is an update of the traditional central patio, providing privacy as well as protection from the sun and rain.

OPPOSITE

A collection of painted polychrome Catholic saints is displayed in the front sitting room.

—

BELOW

The cozy library is a deeply personal space—akin to a portrait of the owner—displaying works by Tomás Esson, Sandu Darie, and Conrado Massaguer, plus other artists Alexis has known in his life.

The Family Home Individually Repurposed
Havana's Home Restaurants

Until recently, the only way Cubans could move from one home to another was via the permuta, or property exchange—a long and complicated process. Raúl Castro's 2011 reforms legalized the buying and selling of houses, leading to the birth of a Havana real estate market, with new websites and agents serving both buyers and homeowners. As a result, the city's choice neighborhoods have recently been dotted with renovations of houses built before the Revolution and repurposed by individuals as bars, restaurants, and guesthouses.

These new private enterprises are the successors of the *paladares*, or home restaurants, that were authorized during the crisis of the 1990s, when the Soviets withdrew their economic aid from Cuba and local authorities were desperate to improve living conditions for citizens. Those early spaces were inventively decorated with whatever was at hand, from old clocks and typewriters to religious figures, kitschy paintings, and mismatched furniture.

Today, the design of these establishments is being used to distinguish them from the competition—signaling

a return to a more personalized Cuban style after fifty years of anonymous state-run businesses. The more interesting of these new businesses are acting as catalysts for neighborhood development—and can be seen as harbingers of a Havana aesthetic of the future. These stylish new interiors are achieved with great effort—their furniture and decoration, equipment, and even special culinary ingredients are often brought from abroad by family members and loyal customers.

Despite the scarcities and challegnes, both the cuisine and the ambiance of today's *paladares* are vastly more sophisticated than the home-restaurants of the 1990s.

LEFT
La Esperanza's special ambiance is the result of quirky decorations, interesting artwork, and views of the surrounding Miramar garden.

TOP RIGHT
The acrylic Philippe Starck Ghost chairs, a gauzy curtain, a 1950s wall of colored glass, and a vintage chandelier provide contemporary glamour at the waterfront Río Mar.

BOTTOM RIGHT
A corner of the garden at La Cocina de Lilliam, one of the earliest and best-known home restaurants.

The Family Home Individually Repurposed

Presenting Beauty in a Pre-Revolution Setting

The top-floor apartment of a picturesque Spanish-style house overlooking the oceanfront Malecón is an unusual gem whose 1940s Hollywood baroque details remain intact. These glamorous touches create an appropriate backdrop for the owner's freelance business renting formal clothes for the weddings, quinces, and first communions that are the most important occasions in the lives of many Havana residents. Everything needed for these events has been brought here from off the island—representing a significant financial investment on the owner's part.

Imagine the reaction of a bridal party—often working-class families from modest neighborhoods—as their dreams for that big day are made real in this apartment's Old Guard setting. The owner's family has lived in this home since the date of construction, which explains the furniture and architectural details so lovingly preserved. This elegant apartment seems the perfect setting to indulge a bride's or debutante's fantasies, aided by the homeowner, who handles details as varied as the wedding party's shoes.

Many Havana couples marry at one of the state-operated marriage palaces now established in former mansions or social clubs of the Pre-Revolution wealthy, which have been repurposed to serve this collective function. Following the ceremony, the bride and groom often pose for photographs in these ornately decorated spaces or in the backseat of the vintage American convertibles that have become a Havana trademark and that are so popular with foreign tourists visiting Havana today.

PREVIOUS PAGE

A bridal gown and veil are displayed in the living room, which is furnished with an elegant Cuban-made Rococo Revival suite of furniture.

———

BELOW LEFT

The dining room's décor is unchanged since the 1950s—here a glamorous painted wood console table complements an ornate wall panel displaying Chinese porcelains on carved brackets.

BELOW RIGHT

The dining table and pleather-covered chairs are arranged ensuite with the console table and unexpectedly illuminated by a 1950s Sputnik chandelier.

BELOW
Men's suits and dress shoes are displayed in one
of the bedrooms, where original furniture includes
mid-century club chairs and a series of antique
Chinese pieces.

2
International Elites and Foreign Diplomats

At the time of the Revolution, there were dozens of international ambassadors posted to Havana, living in the grand official residences their countries owned or rented from the city's elite families.

Today the British, French and Spanish ambassadors, among others, live in the mansions their predecessors had occupied before the 1959 Revolution. The majority of Havana's hundred-odd foreign ambassadors rent their top diplomats' residences from Palco, the state agency that manages a portfolio of state-confiscated houses in the city's exclusive neighborhoods. The size and appearance of these ambassador's residences vary greatly—including the Venetian Gothic palazzo occupied by the French ambassador, the pictur-esque mansion of Argentina's top diplomat, and the mid-century modern villa occupied by the Sri Lankan ambassador. Palco manages dozens of grand houses that today embody the essence of the surrounding historic neighborhood and connect the visitor to Havana's bygone glamour. Most foreign consulates and embassies are also located in former mansions, with many of these found in the Miramar neighborhood.

Several residences—like the Norwegian ambassa-dor's—perform an important cultural function in the city today. Here, the Cuban visitor lucky enough to be invited is introduced to international design trends and to world-class standards of entertaining. These houses showcase national design identity in a historic Havana setting—providing an appropriate backdrop for important cultural dialogue.

Spain has been an important presence in Cuban public life throughout the twentieth century and today their diplomats serve a sizeable community of Spanish investors and executives living in Havana. Houses like the British and the Swiss residences are internationally celebrated works of architecture and are part of every design tourist's wish list of Havana structures to visit. Many residences display some of the original owners' furniture and decorations—preserving a connection to the world interrupted by the Cuban Revolution.

Every four years, a new ambassador to Cuba is appointed by the world's powers. In addition to their work responsibilities, these diplomatic postings involve moving into an official residence, where the recently arrived ambassador might inherit his predecessor's tastes (as well as building problems left behind). Repairs are normally handled by the Palco agency, but these are often sloppy and take seemingly forever to occur. Most new arrivals are content to live with the status quo and leave major repairs for a future diplomat to fix down the line.

The Norwegian Ambassador's Residence

The Norwegian ambassador's residence is a home that satisfies the professional as well as personal functions of a diplomat's house. The residence works equally well for entertaining hundreds of official guests or hosting casual dinners served to a handful of local friends and international houseguests. Invitations to the Norwegian parties are coveted by members of Havana's diplomatic, cultural, artistic, and business worlds. Many ordinary Cubans, who have never traveled off the island, have been exposed to international design styles here for the first time.

The striking decoration of the house was created by Francisco A. Cabrera Gatell—the husband of Ambassador John Petter Opdahl—who in weaving together original 1950s details with his new décor has given the house a personality perfectly in sync with the building's mid-century architecture. Local identity is imparted by the contemporary artwork—much of it Cuban—and the island-made, mid-century furniture. The style is light, bright, airy, colorful, and shelter-magazine sophisticated.

Norway is active in sponsoring a variety of cultural activities in Cuba and in funding scholarships and residencies back home. The couple entertain often—and know what is needed to make the residence work, both in protecting a sense of privacy and in welcoming crowds into the home. In addition, this is one of the rare Havana houses with special care given to the garden, which is usually the setting for the couple's entertainments. Colorful crotons, leafy palms, and grass-like bamboo have recently been planted around the newly built outdoor sitting area—in time this landscape will also be part of the couple's Havana design legacy.

PREVIOUS PAGE

A distinctly Cuban, mid-century console table displays Scandinavian glass, with a painting by Alejandro Campins.

BELOW

Sleek lounge chairs, Neoclassical side tables, and inventive light fixtures surround the pool. In the rear is the recently completed guest bath wing that is used during outdoor entertainments.

BELOW

Clean-lined European upholstered pieces, a pair of
Charles Eames–style plywood chairs, and an impressive
collection of art make the Norwegian ambassador's
residence the most contemporary interior in
Havana today.

NEXT PAGE

Pepe lounges in a recently completed porch addition
that has become the popular spot for entertaining.

The Homes of Havana's Foreign Ambassadors

A survey of Havana's foreign diplomats' residences is a showcase of the most significant architectural styles of the first half of the twentieth century, bearing witness to a sophistication in architecture and interior décor that existed at the time of the 1959 Revolution. From grand houses designed to make a statement at the street, to more informal family homes and including daring works of architectural patronage, the island's most prestigious architecture firms devised houses in the many styles of architecture popular internationally during the first half of the 20th Century, working in whatever esthetic their clients requested.

In most cases, the original properties surrounding these mansions have survived—somewhat neglected, yet unchanged—providing an opportunity to appreciate the interaction between the architecture and the landscape that is such an important element in the authentic Cuban home. These all include covered terraces and other indoor-outdoor spaces where families—then as well as now—spend most of their time.

LEFT

The Swiss ambassador's residence is a perfect integration of International Style, modernism, and tropical landscape.

TOP RIGHT

Josef Frank armchairs are upholstered in fabrics of his design, combining a tropical palette with simple classicism at the Swedish ambassador's house.

BOTTOM RIGHT

Rafael de Cárdenas's Mediterranean-style house, designed for glamorous Americans Grant and Jane Mason, is today the Canadian Ambassador's Residence.

British Ambassador's Residence

The British Ambassador's Residence contains one of Havana's most photographed spaces—the indoor swimming pool wing added to the house and known as the Roman bath of the Mendoza family. The house had been built in 1916 for Pablo Gonzalez de Mendoza by architect Leonard Morales on Avenida Paseo, an important landscaped avenue in Vedado. The house is one of the landmarks for design tourists visiting Havana—with countless requests to visit from international tour groups.

The house has functioned as a diplomatic residence since 1934, when the owner rented it first to the Italian and then to the Soviet Legation. Britain's ambassadors to Cuba have occupied the house since 1957. In its day the house pioneered an integration of the interior and extensive gardens, porches, and terraces. Today, family as well as official life centers on the open-air loggia connecting the public rooms to the pool house and commanding views of the gardens all around.

Brazilian Ambassador's Residence

Next door to the Swedish ambassador's home on the former "Gran Bulevard" of the Country Club is the Brazilian ambassador's residence, with its unique butterfly floorplan centering a curved mass between wings projecting to the right and left. The house is a successful adaptation of Beverly Hills style classicism of the 1940s transported to Havana's premier neighborhood—the work of a talented Cuban architect, possibly Rafael de Cardenas. The double-height front hall is a perfect continuation of the impressive front façade—its sensuous stair and baroque railing bringing some of the exterior detailing indoors.

Today, a palm thatch roof extends the original streamlined modern concrete awning of the rear porch. It is an unusually rustic touch given the Bugger Regency elegance of the interior and seems to convey a sense of Brazilian informality.

Argentine Ambassador's Residence

The Argentine ambassador's Spanish Renaissance–style house was built in 1931 for Ramon Crusellas, the largest manufacturer of soaps and laundry detergents in Cuba. The heavily ornamented exterior is a picturesque composition of towers, balconies and arches that sums up an eclectic, self-confident era on the island. The interior was also meant to impress with its sequence of richly decorated spaces, each with their distinctive multicolored marble floors and ornate coffered ceilings.

The Art Deco–style dining room is an example of the eclectic tastes of Havana's wealthy homeowners—illustrating the Cuban capacity for updating existing spaces in a fashionable contemporary style. Especially seductive are the outdoor spaces that rise out of the lush tropical garden, making the house feel mysterious and romantic. The residence is set back from the street behind a beautiful colonial-style wall protecting its privacy. Neighbors include the Russian, Portuguese, and Slovakian ambassadors.

Dutch Ambassador's Residence

The Dutch Ambassador's Residence is an unusual Arts and Crafts–style bungalow with clay-tiled roofs and dormers that recalls the houses built for the executives who ran American sugar mills found throughout Cuba in the 1920s. The residence has just been given a complete overhaul—including the structure, roof-framing, stairs, windows and air-conditioning system—probably one of the most complex home renovations done in Havana to date. The new pool and stone-clad pool house anchor the residence and define a series of new spaces in the garden. Today's interiors feel brand new—an unusual sensation in Havana, where everything no matter how well-kept sports a certain patina. The black and white kitchen imported from Ikea is the talk of Havana's international community.

German Ambassador's Residence

For the student of Cuban architecture, the German Ambassador's Residence is an iconic house. Built in 1954 for a member of the Fowler Rum family, the American antebellum–style residence is modeled on Tara, the house featured in *Gone With the Wind*. Six double-height wood columns support a horizontal frieze and define the front porch, whose steps span the full width of the front façade. The paneled front door is framed in the classic American colonial manner, while shutters adorn second-story windows as well as the pairs of French doors leading out to the porch. There is nothing else in the city like this anomalous plantation house—which in eclectic Havana feels completely appropriate because of the climate. Just blocks away and equally at home is the house modeled on the Grand Trianon that was built by another member of the Fowler clan. The signature of the German Ambassador's Residence is the elliptical staircase that seems to float on the white marble floor of a front hall decorated with dove-gray Chinese export wallpaper.

Italian Ambassador's Residence

Set back on Miramar's landscaped Fifth Avenue is a 1920s eclectic-style house that is the Italian Ambassador's Residence. The house and its next door neighbor are probably the work of Havana architects Govantes y Cabarrocas, builders of some of the most important Sugar Boom–era houses. The solid yet picturesque massing of towers, projecting balconies, open-air loggias, and single-story wings—is unified by the use of lacy ironwork at all openings. A small terrace, extending the front door out to meet the arriving visitor, is raised up above the circular driveway.

Once inside the elegant front hall, an elaborate marble stair with bold ironwork railing leads to a curved landing defined by an unexpected arch-topped colonnade, with a colorful stained glass window lighting the glamorous stair. Throughout the house, distinctive marble and terrazzo floors in several patterns and color schemes provide interest while keeping the spaces cool.

Spanish Ambassador's Residence

The 1920s were a time of massive Spanish immigration to Cuba and Havana's social clubs representing the peninsula's provinces are reminders of the success achieved by members of that community. Historically, the Spanish ambassador to Cuba has been an important member of Havana's social life—often a titled personage who became the darling of local elite. Since the 1990s, Spain's ambassadors have represented a community of Spanish investors who are stakeholders in hundreds of companies operating in Cuba, including important hotel chains like Melia and Iberostar. Since 2008, the Cuban-born children and grandchildren of Spanish citizens have been awarded more than 60,000 passports as part of the "Grandchildren's Law."

Spain's ambassadors live in an eclectic style house designed in the 1930s by Cuban master Leonardo Morales for the patriarch of the Ward family—the American owners of bakeries and cafeterias in Havana famous for their birthday cakes. Distinctive overhangs of the glazed green-tile roofs are supported by brackets, giving the home the suggestion of an oversized bungalow. This has been the Spanish Ambassador's Residence since the 1950s, when the house was purchased from the builders' family by Spain. This kind of outright ownership of a residence is extremely unusual.

The house is wrapped in shaded porches where the family spends much of their time today. Arches frame views of the extensive gardens with their famed collection of towering royal palms said to be the largest in the city. These anchor the pool and the circular pool house and bar that seem to sum up the glamour of the city's Pre-Revolution lifestyle.

The French Ambassador's Residence

For years, invitations to Havana's French Ambassador's Residence had been notoriously hard to come by. Recent ambassadors have been more welcoming, sharing their mansion, a Cuban architectural icon built for Estanislao del Valle, one of four brothers who were heirs to a historic sugar fortune. This Miramar home was designed in 1930 by prolific Havana architect Rafael de Cárdenas. While one brother, Ignacio, built his Spanish Neoclassical style home across the street (today the residence of the Mexican ambassador), another brother, Javier, built in the Cuban colonial style on a generous lot on the Country Club district (page 176). Estanislao was a deeply religious man, and his home features a wood-paneled library that doubles as a chapel, with Gothic-style ogee arches, armorial stained glass, and a niche displaying a somber, Mannerist painting of Christ descended from the cross.

The mood of the French residence is distinctly European—not just the architectural setting, but the contemporary decorating touches that inject a jolt of color and Gallic flair, confirming the presence of a professional designer. The soaring living room with its wood-beamed ceiling, fanciful iron chandeliers, and château-style fireplace seems appropriately French, as does the Louis XV seating spread throughout. An oversize arched opening connects this salon to the elegant dining room, whose Renaissance-style furniture and antique tapestries convey a cozy Old World feeling. Since the eighteenth century, Cuba has looked to France for cultural inspiration in music, fashion, philosophy, and the arts. Today, the French pieces furnishing the residence seamlessly connect to the Cuban colonial furniture that remains from the original owner's décor.

The ground-floor porch is a generously proportioned space that connects to the principal rooms while extending out into the garden. It is decorated with the original Gothic-style lanterns and unusual wall planters that depict fronds of tropical ironwork framing the doors to the living room. For decades, this monumental porch was the setting for the del Valle family's special occasions as well as their everyday family gatherings. Today, this shaded space remains at the center of both daily life and diplomatic entertainments—an example of the indoor-outdoor living that is Havana style at its most successful.

PREVIOUS PAGE

Contemporary wicker furniture in natural tones is arranged on the garden loggia—a comfortable update of the space's original outdoor seating.

OPPOSITE

The iconic rear elevation, an adaptation of the Venetian Gothic Cà d'Zan, defines a generous arcaded porch overlooking the garden at both the upper and lower levels.

BELOW LEFT

The ambience of the dining room is elegant yet intimate, a cozy contrast to the monumentally scaled living room.

BELOW RIGHT

A screen of ogee arches in the front hall anchor the marble stair rising to the second floor, providing both drama and privacy.

3

State Rentals in Exclusive Neighborhoods

Fidel's confidant Celia Sánchez Manduley is credited with assembling a pool of expropriated mansions and repurposing them as VIP guesthouses and diplomatic residences.

Beginning in 1960s with four houses in the Country Club district, today the state controls more than 100 official guesthouses—including a dozen beach houses—in some of Havana's most high-security areas. The Palco agency handles the operation of these casas de protocolo, or diplomatic guesthouses, where the members of the Communist Party elite from the days of Soviet Bloc delegations were housed and officially entertained. A list of the former owners of Palco's houses is a who's who of Pre-Revolution Havana's wealthiest families: Gomez Mena, Aguilera, Falla, Suero, Santeiro, Tarafa, Fanjul, and Batista. The Palco portfolio includes examples of all the significant architectural styles of the first half of the twentieth century designed by Cuba's most respected architects.

Most of Cuba's foreign residents—a New Guard of expats, businessmen, and diplomatic staff who have lived on the island for decades—occupy rentals managed by Palco, which also provides services to foreign firms and embassies.

Although these houses are more architecturally interesting than the condominium apartments recently constructed for Havana's foreigners their maintenance can be challenging. Many of these international tenants choose to foot the bill for improvements like adding a swimming pool or providing modern comforts that

outsiders take for granted. These long-term foreign residents have created very personalized houses—places where children are brought up, local friends are entertained, and foreign guests are invited to enjoy a warm-weather holiday. Among the residents of these state-owned houses are Cubans who live internationally and feel fortunate to have recaptured the sense of having a Havana home—something they felt had been lost forever.

Palco also coordinates short-term rentals, providing international tourists with spacious, fully staffed vacation homes. Renting one of these suburban villas is a unique opportunity for the visitor to experience the Pre-Revolution lifestyle of the elite Havana neighborhoods rarely visited by tourists today.

Raising a Family
Katharina Voss & Enrique Arias

Most foreign residents in Havana live in the city for a limited amount of time while performing a particular job or filling a diplomatic post. For the past fifteen years, this international couple—she's German, he's the the descendant of prominent Cuban family—and their three children have made this 1950s house their Havana home. Trained as an architect and the daughter of one, Katharina's design background is apparent in the series of transformations made to the home they rent from the Palco agency. Like many expats, the couple have made a variety of improvements at their own expense—including the swimming pool, which is a focus of the lushly landscaped garden.

The flow of the house, an open plan of intimately scaled spaces, was respected as the renovation progressed. Changes include the creation of a combination TV and sitting room and the addition of a spacious thatch-roofed, open-air terrace that works beautifully for large parties as well as for family intimacy, embodying the best of Cuban outdoor living.

Katharina's special sensibility combines 1950s furniture and the works of promising young Cuban artists whom the couple have come to know, resulting in a comfortable, contemporary ambiance. Cuban woodworkers fabricate custom pieces—like the massive outdoor dining table—when the wife can't find these items ready-made. Although these spaces are comfortable year-round, the family avoids the worst of the summer heat on the island by decamping to visit family abroad. The decoration feels young, comfortable, and confident with its mix of good pieces and serious art—celebrating the informality of living in Cuba and the spontaneity of making the best of whatever is at hand.

LEFT
A collection of whimsical cut-glass candlesticks adorns the alfresco dining area, which is centered on the Cuban mahogany table fabricated to Katharina's design.

PREVIOUS PAGE, LEFT

In the intimately scaled sitting room, mid-century Cuban armchairs frame a painting by Alejandro Campins.

PREVIOUS PAGE, RIGHT

A sculpture adds humor to the swimming pool nestled in the tropical landscape of the rear garden.

BELOW

Mid-century chairs surround a distinctly Cuban glass table on a biomorphic wood base in the more formal interior dining area.

OPPOSITE

Cushions are accents of bright color in the otherwise neutral corner porch. A metal sphere sculpture by Damian Aquiles hangs at the center of a suite of vintage pieces, including a 1920s Cuban rocker.

The Former Pollack, Humara, Tarafa, Kaffenburg, and Noval Houses

Since the 1970s the Palco agency has been expanding its role by providing a variety of additional services, so that the Palco Enterprise Group was launched in 2011. The new entity continues to be in charge of providing housing for foreign diplomats and Havana's international residents renting out more than 1,500 houses and apartments.

Following the re-establishment of relations between Cuba and the US, the number of foreign embassies in Havana has grown and Palco has found homes for staff members and official residences for those new ambassadors. The group runs an employment agency where local personnel for embassies and diplomatic residences are vetted and hired. Palco is even involved in the operation of the schools for the children of Havana's foreign residents.

Before the arrival of AirBnb or the government sanctioned bed-and-breakfasts or *casas particulares*, Palco's repurposed mansions were the place where official tourists were received and entertained. With Palco in charge of staffing, catering, security—not to mention the often hit-and-miss decoration of these historic structures. The Palco portfolio includes Pre-Revolution houses designed by Havana's best known architects in every imaginable twentieth century style. Five years ago, international visitors could easily book a short stay in these landmark mansions. This seems to have become more difficult as international demand for these unique accommodations has increased.

Palco is now heavily involved in the tourist industry: identifying prime development sites in the city where it will renovate existing buildings or construct new high-end structures. The organization is in charge of logistics for the 100-odd international conferences and trade shows that take place annually in facilities like the Havana Pabexpo and the International Conference Center. In addition to running every detail of those events, Palco is responsible for the accommodations required by attendees. The group also offers party planning and catering, all kinds of support services related to international congresses: including printing, translation, transportation, and shipping.

House of Mark Pollack

ABOVE

The garden loggia of the Pollack house, extending
the beautifully detailed interior out into the
surroundings, is a space that is welcoming at all
times of day.

House of the Humara
y Maderne Family

ABOVE

Recalling a traditional Cuban courtyard, the double
staircase of the Humara y Maderne house is set in a
double-height volume surrounded by classical arcades.

House of Antonio Tarafa

ABOVE
Set behind a distinctive stone wall, the house combines classicism with eclectic massing and details.

House of José Noval Cueto

LEFT
At the center of the garden elevation is a dramatic volume that evokes the courtyard of Havana's historic houses.

PREVIOUS PAGES, LEFT
During his 1940s visit to Havana, Walter Gropius pronounced the house of José Noval Cueto his favorite work of contemporary Cuban design.

PREVIOUS PAGES, TOP RIGHT
The master bedroom of the Mark Pollack house has been decorated with Italian eighteenth-century-style pieces, suiting its role in receiving VIP guests.

PREVIOUS PAGES, BOTTOM RIGHT
A side porch of the Beaux Arts–style Humara y Maderne house overlooks the extensive garden.

House of Albert Kaffenburg

TOP LEFT
The clay tile roof of the pool house is a traditional detail amid the mature tropical landscape.

Recovering a Sense of the Lost Home
Ella Cisneros

The Cuban-born, Venezuela-based art collector who recently renovated this house has recovered a home in Havana and decorated it with a glamour and comfort that reflects her personality—transporting a bit of Bel Air to the Cuban capital. Ella Cisneros' sprawling house was built by José "Pepe" Gómez-Mena—the owner of sugar mills, distilleries, and extensive real estate—for his second wife, Elizarda Sampedro. Before creating this informal, streamlined Art Moderne home, Pepe had previously built the city's most elegant Louis XV–style mansion for wife number one in the Vedado.

The Gomez-Mena house was constantly being transformed by party decorators. Their 1948 dinner for King Leopold of Belgium featured a banquet table that wrapped around the swimming pool and culminated in the draperies of the royal box, where the crowned heads were on display. Following the Revolution, the Gómez-Mena house was expropriated and became known simply as *casa numero cinco*, a diplomatic guesthouse where the most important international visitors to Havana were entertained.

Two years ago, Cisneros rented this house from Palco and it is once again the site of memorable parties, especially those celebrating events in Havana's art scene. The house today displays a cohesive, tasteful glamour that is unique in the city. Comfortable upholstery is balanced with Anglo-Indian furniture and Spanish Colonial antiques, which in turn are played off Cuban Pop and abstract paintings from Cisneros' contemporary and modern collections. The decoration has recaptured the seamless integration of the elegant interiors with the distinctive pool and the surrounding gardens that was a hallmark of houses of Havana's Pre-Revolution social elite.

While extraordinary hosts like the Norwegian ambassador will depart at the end of their Havana postings, Ella Cisneros is set to remain in her native city, a generous supporter of culture and an important social force. She is one of a small but growing number of Cuban exiles who have found, once again, the haven of a home in Havana, something she had once thought had been lost to her forever.

PREVIOUS PAGE
An Italian giltwood side chair and one of a pair of Neoclassical chandeliers complement an important Sandu Darie painting from the 1950s.

———

OPPOSITE
A view of the garden is framed by the columns of the generous porch that serves as a transition space between the interiors and the surrounding landscape.

BELOW LEFT
A sculpture by Rita Longa anchors the end of the swimming pool and is a focal point from the interior of the streamlined modern-style house.

———

BELOW RIGHT
The sinuous stair to the bedroom floor is lit by an oversize window, the walls hung with Cuban pieces ranging from vintage 1950s to contemporary works.

NEXT PAGE
The living room's stylish mix includes antique English furniture, a Spanish Colonial bench, a 1961 Pop art painting by Umberto Peña and a Lolo Soldevilla sculpture on the cocktail table.

4

Havana's Artistic Elite

While foreigners living in state-owned houses constitute an international elite in Havana, Cuba's artists are themselves an exclusive group, occupying a place of privilege in the Cuban economy.

Throughout the twentieth century, Havana enjoyed a thriving art scene, especially in the 1940s and 1950s when Cuban artists returned from their studies abroad and energized the local art world by introducing trends then popular in Paris and New York. During the Revolution, visual artists performed an important role, creating posters, exhibitions, and installations that celebrated social goals and political accomplishments. Since 1984, Havana has hosted an international art biennial, showcasing local artists while presenting the work of unrecognized Third World creators. Contemporary Cuban art has developed an international following with foreign collectors on the lookout for fresh works at galleries, auction houses, and international art fairs. Havana's affluent homeowners comprise a lively group of collectors and patrons, interested in acquiring blue-chip pieces as well as works fresh off the easel.

Cuban law permits artists to sell their work to foreigners, while the US embargo has always allowed Americans to purchase art on the island as part of an approved cultural exchange. This has made Havana's artists among the most affluent members of the island's population—ironic as artists around the world struggle to earn a living.

Cuban artists have invested in home studios where they live and work—often receiving groups of foreign visitors brought to them by international curators or local tour guides. This art tourism allows foreign visitors to experience firsthand how Cubans—albeit the creative elite—live in Havana today. Most of these spaces are family homes that have been repurposed as commercial enterprises where the entire family is busy delivering supplies, packing artwork, selling catalogs, or serving snacks to visitors.

As might be expected, Havana's artists' spaces boast a highly individual style and an authentic Cuban essence while reflecting the international experiences many of these creators have enjoyed abroad.

Recently, successful Cuban artists are returning to Havana after working and exhibiting internationally for years, leaving behind studio spaces in places like Brooklyn or Madrid and making a commitment to be a part of this next phase in the island's history, encouraged by the thaw in diplomatic relations with the United States.

Individual Style, International Profile

Carlos Quintana

The painter Carlos Quintana has a reputation as an outspoken member of Havana's contemporary art scene. The mostly self-taught artist has enjoyed international acclaim with exhibitions in the United States, Europe, Latin America, and China. His mystical paintings—with Sufis, samurais, and buddhas floating over gestural brushstrokes—hang in the homes of Havana's cultural elite. Each painting conveys a different feeling within the individual residential contexts. Quintana spends part of each year in Spain, where he has a kept a studio since the 1990s. It is a far cry from the miniscule service room at the back of an encouraging aunt's apartment that served as his first art-making space. Throughout his career, the role of the studio where he does his painting has had a special significance for him.

Today, Quintana lives and works in a streamlined Art Moderne duplex set on a quiet cul-de-sac in Havana's upscale Kohly neighborhood. He paints in several spaces of the building—including the front porch, which often serves as a place for packing works heading off to international exhibitions. Quintana hopes to convert the rear of the house into administrative and work spaces in order to move the making and selling of the art out of the intimacy of his home. In the meantime, those who follow his creations internationally feel fortunate to visit him in these spaces where the intimacy of his personal life and his artistic creativity are equally on display.

LEFT
A recent painting by Carlos Quintana is hung behind a 1950s Cuban armchair. On the low table is a clay sculpture also by the artist.

Art Tourism in a Mid-Century Gem

Estudio de 7ma y 60

The space that photographer María Cienfuegos shares with two other artists is not exactly a working studio nor is it a home—and it differs from the traditional gallery in that collectors can interact with the artists directly instead of via a dealer or gallery staff.

The ground-floor apartment feels timeless with its mix of traditional Cuban construction elements—simple wood louvers and iron grilles, stained-glass windows, exposed brick walls, and clay tile floors—filtered through an International Style aesthetic. Design connoisseurs recognize the distinctive architecture of group's studio as a master work by Tropical Modernist designer Mario Romañach—an illustration of the search for national identity in architecture that bore fruit in the 1950s. The contemporary artwork and a few well-chosen pieces of stylish furniture are all it takes to make these spaces emblematic of the sophisticated style of Havana today.

LEFT TOP

The studio's eclectic furnishings include a painted wicker rocker pulled up to a Victorian library table. Contemporary photographs hang on the exposed brick walls among a setting of colored glass and decorative wood screens.

LEFT BOTTOM

Architect Mario Romañach included several of his aesthetic hallmarks in the design of this apartment building, including a connection between the interiors and the outdoors, generous cross-ventilation and exposed construction materials.

A Cabinet of Curiosities
JEFF

Artist José Emilio Fuentes Fonseca, aka JEFF, is fascinated with themes related to childhood, incorporating toy sailboats, trains, and buses in work that has often been labeled naïve or "outsider." JEFF lives in a 1950s Vedado apartment building, whose open plan blends the dining room, sitting room, and glassed-in terrace enjoying dramatic views of the city. His flair for interiors can be seen in the interplay between the décor and artwork he has created and displays. The simple seating of the living room, furniture that he designed, is juxtaposed with a Louis XV–style club chair, an intriguing survivor from Havana's glamorous past. Custom-made pieces contrast with examples of *resolviendo*—the Cuban art of making due with whatever is at hand—like the truck tire supporting a glass top that results as a sculptural coffee table.

JEFF is a poster child for the Cuban educational system, which identifies and supports talented children from an early age. As a teenager, he was sent to an elite boarding school where his artistic skills were honed. By the age of twenty, he had his first solo exhibition and received a grant from a prestigious foreign foundation. He has created artistic landscapes as well as an installation depicting a classroom, a reference to that recurring childhood theme. Recently, he is known for the herd of colorfully painted metal elephants he created for the 2009 Havana Biennal—which have been installed in several places in the city to the delight of local residents.

OPPOSITE

The dining room's mismatched collection of chairs
surrounds a mid-century table. JEFF's boldly colorful,
oversize paintings comment on the island's politics in a
naïve visual language.

———

BELOW

The sofa and side chair were designed by JEFF,
who also envisioned the unusual blue and white leather
upholstery used on the 1940s Rococo–style club chair.

Ibrahim Miranda

Painter Ibrahim Miranda is known in Havana as a professor, engraver, and artist with a deep interest in map-making. Since the 1990s, he has traveled almost constantly, showing at international exhibitions, and the recipient of foreign residencies in Europe and the United States. Working with recycled media, Miranda employs map glyphs and cartography to create scroll paintings that explore the vulnerability of living on an island, the isolation of physical limits, and the expansion of borders.

Other important themes in Miranda's art include journeys, geographic locations, and the transformations of a city's layout into the imaginary animals of an urban bestiary. His vibrant sense of color is apparent in acrylic paintings on canvas, silkscreen prints, and works on paper that layer pattern on top of pattern.

Miranda's Vedado apartment is on the ground floor of a small Art Deco building, whose simple spaces are filled with bright light in spite of the painted wood louvers that temper the Cuban sun. His work is everywhere, framed and hung or simply propped up—part archive, part work in progress. The colors and gestures found in his paintings relate to the visual richness of all the works layered one on top of each other throughout the apartment's intimately scaled spaces. In sorting through these works the lucky visitor experiences something of the way Miranda's paintings reveal patterns and identify overarching shapes.

LEFT
Paintings are stacked in a corner of Ibrahim Miranda's office, which is simply furnished with a 1970s table and folding chairs.

Evoking Artists' Lofts Around the World

Wilfredo Prieto

What would one expect the Havana home studio of an internationally recognized Cuban conceptual artist to look like? Wilfredo Prieto once installed a bar of soap, a rotting banana peel, and some bits of axle grease on the floor of the Museo Nacional de Bellas Artes in Havana. For his installation Biblioteca Blanca, Prieto carefully arranged five thousand completely blank books on the shelves lining the four walls of a library. So, how would the apartment of the creator of these abstract pieces define comfort in the home?

The loft-like spaces of Prieto's studio speak to a certain detachment that has made his art universally appealing. Here are found just the necessary elements to eat, sleep, work, and sit. While a certain emptiness might emphasize the poetic quality of the volumes, the light, colors, and vintage furniture are Havana trademarks that connect to his vision of himself as a Cuban artist.

Prieto has recently returned to Havana full-time, leaving behind a studio in New York, a city he claims is no longer as lively as the Cuban capital, where he feels things are really happening. He has renovated

an apartment in a once-elegant Art Deco building, combining spaces and tearing down walls, preserving the distressed wall paint and the traditional Cuban floor tiles. It is refreshing to encounter this minimalist reading of personal comfort—an austerity that makes sense given Wilfredo Prieto's cerebral approach to making art.

Prieto's commitment to Havana's future is illustrated in his recent purchase of an important colonial house—a marvelous wreck that he will renovate as a cultural space. Those who admire the restraint in his art are curious to see how far he'll take the reconstruction.

LEFT
Colorful Cuban floor tiles from the 1920s continue into the open kitchen, which was constructed using locally available materials while incorporating imported appliances.

NEXT PAGE
In the light-filled spaces, assistants field phone calls while working on laptops at mid-century tables—an important part of Wilfred Prieto's creative process is the planning and organization of his installations.

A Home Base in Havana

Dagoberto Rodríguez

In 1995, artists Dagoberto "Dago" Rodríguez, Marco Castillo, and Alexandre Arrechea moved in together after completing their art-school studies in Havana. The trio began work on fantastic conceptual art pieces often executed in Cuba's historic hardwoods. The creation of their internationally successful arts collaborative, known as Los Carpinteros, coincided with the economic crisis of the 1990s that followed the withdrawal of Soviet support to the island and the void left by artists who had abandoned Cuba during the Mariel boatlift of 1980.

In 2009, after an exhibition in Madrid, Dago and Marco took a studio space there; it was a place where they felt they would be more connected to the international art world and more productive. But while life in Madrid was satisfying, the call of Cuba was hard to resist. Following the legalization of real estate transactions in Cuba, the duo purchased a four-story house in Nuevo Vedado, which they are rehabilitating as their Havana studio with spaces for an arts archive, a library, and an exhibition space accessible to students and the community.

Dago's own Havana home is a single-family house in Vedado distinguished by its simple and warm ambiance, jazzed up with the mid-century furniture that always evokes the feeling of Havana. Signs of the artist's elaborate installations and large-scale constructions are nowhere to be seen. An exposed brick wall in the living room contrasts with the white plaster walls and creamy terrazzo floors—recalling loft spaces in Europe or the United States. Drawings and artwork by friends include a sky-blue wheelbarrow sculpture that acts as coffee table.

The dining room and cozy, eat-in kitchen sport mid-century Cuba pieces—nowhere is there a reference to the conceptual installations or the ironic pieces of furniture this artist is known for around the world. At the rear of the house is an extensive garden featuring an antique Spanish fountain splashing in the shade of palm fronds and banana leaves—a calming sound amid the city's bustle, and a Havana oasis for an international figure returned home.

PREVIOUS PAGE

A confetti of mosaic tile unites the kitchen and adjacent breakfast area located at the heart of the house. These have been renovated with flair and furnished with elegant 1950s chairs around a table incorporating a Singer sewing machine base.

———

BELOW LEFT

Mid-century Cuban chairs of a decidedly Italian inspiration surround a 1950s glass-topped dining table—a staple of Havana's stylish houses.

BELOW RIGHT

An antique marble fountain is a focal point of the overgrown rear garden.

———

OPPOSITE

The living room is furnished with contemporary side chairs and an inventive wheelbarrow coffee table, while artwork by friends is hung on the exposed brick walls.

The Revolution's Avant-Garde
Nelson Domínguez

Off one of the most historic squares of Old Havana, overlooking the eighteenth-century convent and church of San Francisco, is the studio and state-run art gallery of painter Nelson Domínguez. At the street level, oversize doors swing open to reveal the shop and exhibition space set up in the traditional warehouse of an eighteenth-century merchant's home. On the second floor—where the original family would have lived—is Domínguez's studio, lit by tall windows commanding views of the church on one side and, on the other, the house's original garden at the rear of the property.

As a boy, Domínguez remembers witnessing the Cuban Revolution from his rural home in the Sierra Maestra mountains near Santiago de Cuba. In the late 1960s he was a student at Cuba's famed Escuelas Nacionales de Arte (National Art Schools), which the new Revolutionary government had opened just years before.

He was named a professor at the art schools, eventually heading their painting department. Domínguez represents the generation of artists preceding the internationally successful creators of the last decades. His talents have been consistently recognized by the Cuban state, which has honored him with membership in Cuba's prestigious national union of writers and artists, and awarded him the Cuban Ministry of Culture's prestigious national art award.

Since his early career, Dominguez' art has been popular in revolutionary circles, as evidenced by the sketches and paintings found throughout the studio of his heroes, prima ballerina Alicia Alonso and the comandante Fidel Castro. Works in progress are found in every corner of his workspace as are a variety of objects that are the ingredients needed for the drawings, ceramics, prints, furniture, sculpture, and paintings he creates in this space. Coincidentally, Domínguez is an accomplished chef, an intuitive creator, and a gracious host, always trying out a new recipe and anxious to share the results.

LEFT
In Nelson Domínguez's historic Old Havana studio, Victorian pieces are in dialogue with his clothespin-backed throne—behind is a balcony overlooking the extensive rear garden.

5

Havana's Tastemakers: the International Influence of Individual Houses

Havana style today can be imagined as a mosaic of the lifestyle narratives of creative homeowners—deeply personal spaces that, when taken together, tell the city's contemporary design story.

With rare exceptions, these homes are the work of self-taught decorators and untrained collectors, their groupings of furniture and artwork evoking memories and engaging the viewer in conversation. Many of these homeowners travel internationally—with some living abroad during part of the year. All of them speak of a longing for their Havana home that is hard to resist when they've been away from the city for long. They crave a refueling of the spirit that can only occur in the Cuban capital.

Havana's tastemakers have transported global design trends and ways of life to their houses while holding on to their home's Cuban essence. In most cases, contemporary Cuban art is employed to revitalize the historic architecture, which is always the context in a city where little new construction has occurred since 1959. The creators of Havana's most personalized houses have fashioned aesthetic worlds of their own, relying on Cuba's celebrated resourcefulness. Authentic Cuban style is accomplished with limited financial resources and despite the scarcity of construction materials resulting from the US embargo and the island's depressed economy. Havana's homes balance personal comfort—historically important in the brutal tropical climate—with a sense of drama that is very Cuban. The authentic Cuban beauty achieved in each of these homes should be understood as the owner's personal triumph over the island's cultural and economic constraints.

Living in Havana Part-Time

Pepe Horta

In the 1990s, Miami's Café Nostalgia pioneered the presentation of contemporary Cuban music as a celebration of vintage island style. Despite the name, it was a forward-looking experience—akin at times to contemporary performance art. The Havana apartment of Pepe Horta, one of Café Nostalgia's founders, is a scrapbook of the owner's memories, with furniture and artwork illustrating his personal trajectory involving time spent in Paris, the club in Miami, and his involvement in Havana's music and culture scene over many years. Pieces of vintage Vuitton luggage are a souvenir of Horta's first trip to France, where he was posted as a cultural attaché, as well as a reminder of the fluidity of the life he enjoys today. Horta spends half his time in Miami, living internationally while holding on to the Cuban identity he expresses in this Havana home, where he was born.

The early twentieth-century apartment displays traditional Cuban architectural details: high ceilings, tiled floors, public rooms that connect via double-height openings, and operable glass transoms allowing air to flow through the bedrooms. The interconnected spaces of this traditional Vedado home give the apartment a loft-like modernity, enhancing Havana's signature pairing of contemporary art with antique Cuban furniture displayed in a historic architectural setting.

Installation pieces created for performances that Horta organized are often pulled from storage and spontaneously propped against one of the apartment's walls. Pieces he has recently acquired also find their way onto the walls—yet these interiors are kept surprisingly uncluttered, allowing the owner to leaf through the memories that make this place his spiritual home.

LEFT
Throughout Havana's history, seating furniture—like these caned colonial rockers—was gathered around a center table placed below a chandelier in the formal salon. This Tiffany-style light fixture is a type that became popular in Havana after the 1959 Revolution.

BELOW LEFT

In the front hall, the antique wicker furniture—
possibly by Heywood-Wakefield—has been
kept unpainted.

———

BELOW RIGHT

The kitchen mixes a colonial-era armoire with acrylic
chairs brought from the United States and arranged
around an Art Deco mahogany pedestal table.

OPPOSITE

Cuban artwork dominates the spacious dining room
with its 1920s classical-style furniture. At right is
a work by Servando Cabrera Moreno, and, at left,
an important piece by Humberto Castro from
the 1980s.

Contemporary Art Revitalizing Historic Architecture
Gretchen & Jean-Marc Ville

———————

It might be surprising to find a Parisian art collector living in Havana's Santos Suárez, an unassuming neighborhood fifteen minutes from the center of town. The businessman and his Cuban wife live in a perfectly preserved Art Deco villa raised above street level and detached from its surroundings by palms and other vegetation wrapping the house on all sides. Cast-stone accents—fluted pilasters, geometric frieze panels, and supporting brackets—give the salmon-colored house a strong identity that continues throughout the interior.

This house invariably produces an emotional response in visitors—a profound sense of well-being. This is coupled with a feeling of discovery as one travels through art-filled spaces, culminating in the dining room, a beautiful and somewhat exotic room. A visit to the house is a special treat for those with a knowledge of Cuban art history. Classic works include a wall of Julio Girona portraits and early canvases by Servando Cabrera Moreno, plus more recent paintings by Manuel Mendive, Alfredo Sosabravo, and Carlos Quintana. The very personal style of this home is reinforced by the unique furniture designed by Jean-Marc using

unusual materials like charred wood beams recycled as benches around the glass-topped dining table.

The house conserves many of the original interior details: ornate plaster moldings, boldly patterned floor tiles, latticework windows and doors, and colorful period bathrooms—all suggesting that everything was found intact, which belies the owner's extensive efforts at restoration. Havana's historic houses are living organisms requiring constant attention—from replacing the glazing putty of the windows to restoring woodwork suffering from humidity and the unrelenting sun. Gretchen and Jean-Marc see themselves as custodians of an important architectural legacy. Although this is clearly the home of serious art collectors, the couple's understated personal style is front and center, creating European comfort in an ambiance that feels authentically Cuban.

———————

LEFT
In the living room, a puzzle table anchors a grouping of inventive sofa and chairs with plywood arms and simple black leather cushions—all pieces designed by Jean-Marc.

BELOW LEFT

Simple bookcases line the walls of the office, displaying reference books as well as a variety of Cuban works on paper from the 1960s.

———

BELOW RIGHT

The central hall with its enfilade of Moorish arches and ceiling cornices decorated with Arabic script is an unexpected touch of fantasy in an otherwise strictly Art Deco interior.

OPPOSITE

The subtle textures and somber palette of the dining room artwork—including a painting by Roberto Diago—can be appreciated in this light-filled space.

Juan Carlos Martínez & Michel Báez

This gracious apartment in a gritty part of Old Havana tells a very Cuban story—of traditional layouts, extended family living, and the courtyard at the heart of the family's daily activities. The home sits on the second floor, above a former commercial space that, historically, would have been owned by the family living above the shop. In the nineteenth-century manner, public rooms and bedrooms are distributed around the patio, with the dining room and service areas located at the rear of the building. This once-popular housing type is rarely encountered in Havana nowadays and represents a vanishing element of the city's architectural past.

Today, this house celebrates hospitality and traditions. Despite the owners' lack of formal training and their youth, they have surrounded themselves with a solid collection of Cuban decorative arts displayed to great advantage in the apartment's historic context. Just as in the past—before the use of air-conditioning—family members seek the shade throughout different areas of the interior as the sun works its way around the home.

Members of the couple's social set gather here for *tertulias*, discussions of events in the city's cultural life, just as their ancestors did in Havana a century ago. The house is distinctive for its bold use of color as for the attention paid to service spaces like the charmingly decorated kitchen and bath.

As in the homes of design buffs everywhere, things are always in flux in order to accommodate the latest purchase. The couple often repair their acquisitions themselves. Recently, they have even tried their hand at upholstery in yet another example of the ingenuity required in Cuba for an owner to create and maintain a stylish home.

PREVIOUS PAGE
The colorful entrance hall connects to the staircase and the central patio. Traditional details include the *mamparas* or low doors, stained-glass fanlights, and the exuberant palette of the tile floors.

———

OPPOSITE
Pastries are presented on crystal stands in the dining room—an opportunity to show off the couple's collections of antique porcelain and silverware.

BELOW
More formal furniture is arranged in the street-front parlor, whose louvered doors are kept closed to muffle the sounds of the city and maintain privacy from the neighbors across the way.

Jorge Perugorría & Elsa María Lafuente

To the west of Havana, past the international yachts anchored at Marina Hemingway, is the former fishing village of Santa Fe, where rustic bungalows recall the Cuban countryside. At the time of the Revolution, this area was being developed with the construction of boat slips, a small hotel, and a handful of modernist houses that pioneered a waterfront lifestyle still somewhat unusual in the city.

Jorge "Pichi" Perugorría, Cuba's most famous leading man, and his childhood sweetheart, Elsa María "Elsita" Lafuente, have brought up their three sons in one of these seaside houses, which they have transformed over the years with the addition of new spaces to accommodate their growing family. This deceptively simple 1950s house is architecturally unusual, with elevated areas, a theatrical framing of vistas, and built-in cabinetry used to define areas within the open plan.

The couple lives surrounded by a lifetime of mementos, including international awards and the posters of the husband's movies in foreign titles—reminders of his work with legendary directors like Tomás Gutiérrez

Alea, Steven Soderbergh, and Bigas Luna. In spite of their glamorous travels, both confess that the pull of their Havana home has always been hard to resist.

Pichi and Elsita's house has always been a significant cultural salon in Havana, where international friends are welcomed, films are edited in the studio, or the sons are recording music in the extensive waterfront garden. It is easy to see why their parties—especially their annual New Year's Eve bash—are legendary among Havana's creative class. Recently, the couple has opened an art gallery in an part of Old Havana that is off the beaten track—working with the local community in their development and renovation plans and joining the handful of Havana tastemakers who have been investing in the city's cultural scene.

PREVIOUS PAGE

The dining room is raised above the living area and
framed by floating bookshelves, giving the space a
theatrical feel.

————

BELOW

The sculptural stair floats within the interlocking
double-height volumes of the interiors—which are
defined by block walls and exposed concrete ceilings.

OPPOSITE

An idyllic view from the waterfront backyard
of the private dock and some residential islands just
beyond, setting the tone for the informality of
the interiors.

NEXT PAGE
Music-making centers around the grand piano at
one end of the living room. At right, a painting by
Carlos Quintana hangs above a rustic bamboo
settee commissioned by Elsita.

115

Transporting International Lifestyle to the Tropics

Carlos Ferreira

Many of Cuba's high-end tourist hotel interiors—including Havana's Parque Central and the Saratoga—have been designed by Carlos Ferreira, a Spanish architect who has been working on the island for decades. His commercial designs have captured a sophisticated Cuban style for the broad market while remaining reassuringly international. The Miramar home he rents from Palco features a very personal mixture of European antiques, Cuban colonial furniture, and contemporary art installed with a dramatic flair. The flowing interiors of his mid-century house seem to have been created for entertaining, which often occurs in the garden Carlos shares with his Rhodesian Ridgebacks and Jack Russell terriers.

The house was a wreck when Carlos first saw it, including a roof that was mostly missing. He wasn't put off by the challenge and embarked on a reclamation that included adding a new pool and substantial landscaping of the garden. The simplicity of the interior architecture—interconnected volumes, windows bringing the outdoors in, milky terrazzo floors, and white painted spaces—is a neutral canvas on which Carlos arranges his treasures. Everywhere you look are

works by Cuba's blue-chip contemporary artists and furniture that includes some fine Art Deco pieces that Carlos acquired during his years in London. The décor is international yet completely grounded in Cuba—but it is the display and arrangement that set it apart.

Carlos continues decorating Cuba's top-end hotels while working on personal projects associated with the new optimistic mood of today's Havana. These include La Reserva, an intimately scaled new boutique hotel in historic Vedado that is certain to be a success. The "La Reserva experience" reflects Carlos's encyclopedic knowledge of Havana's historic architecture—setting the bar high for other island designers looking to provide sophisticated international visitors with an authentically Cuban guest experience.

LEFT
The mosquito net surrounding the master bed feels both historically Cuban and dramatically romantic.

NEXT PAGE
The double-height living room is centered on a large fireplace, an unusual feature in Havana. The adjacent dining room, which appears to be perched above it, connects to the sunlit gallery and garden beyond.

BELOW LEFT

A pair of 1950s upholstered chairs, recalling the work of Harry Bertoia, and an unusual standing lamp, displayed with a work by Agustín Bejarano.

———

BELOW RIGHT

A marble-topped Cuban colonial dressing table is placed at the guest bedroom window, which is framed in colorful chintz curtains.

OPPOSITE

The neoclassical-style sideboard features an unusual decoration of brass tacks and is flanked by Italian side chairs and a charming painting of Caribbean life.

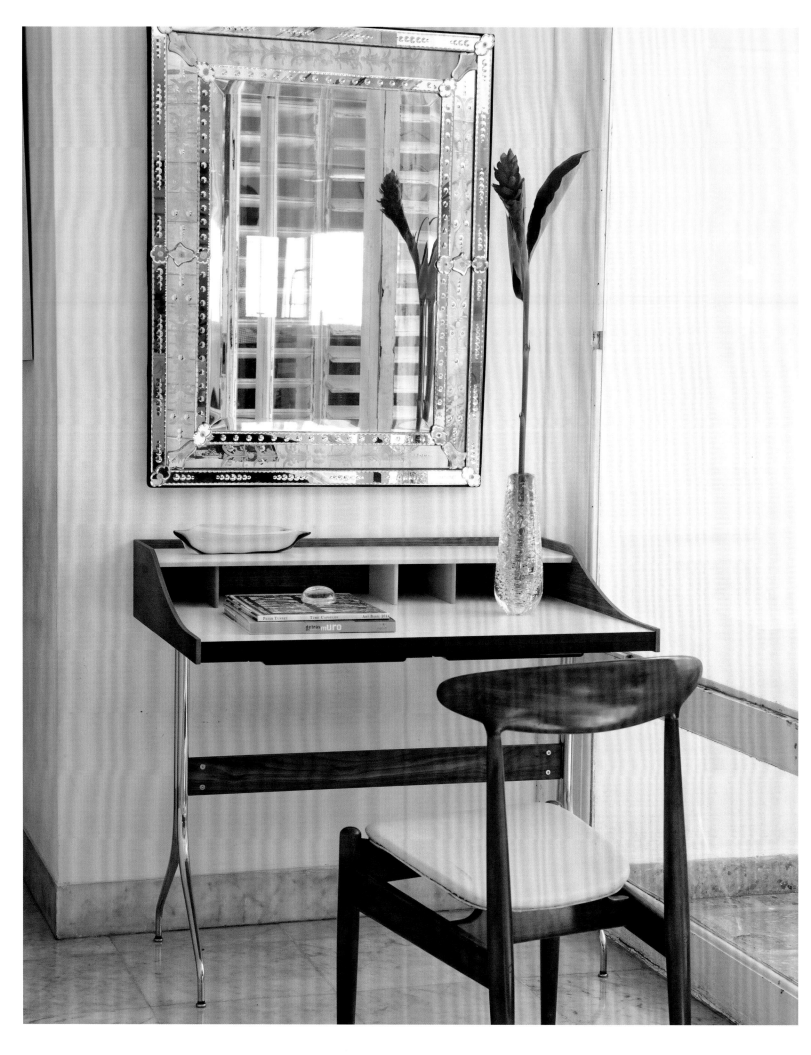

The Novelty of Practicing Restraint
Mid-Century Modern in the Western Suburbs

The owner of this house is an exotic beauty, a model who was popular during the 1990s when international fashion photographers discovered Cuba's unspoiled allure, romantically decaying architecture, and stunning women. Since then she has been appearing in music videos, plays, and telenovelas, all while bringing up her young daughter in her mid-century Havana home. Her astute eye—the consequence of her days in front of the camera—has been brought to bear on the creation of these simple yet stylish interiors.

The house is on a large property behind a garden wall on a busy street of the suburban Biltmore area. Surprises include an unusual open-air entry court that brings the tropical surroundings into the interior of the house, creating a graceful transition from the city's bustle to the intimacy of the home.

The simple light-filled interiors display a casual marriage of 1950s architecture with exactly the types of pieces that could have been part of the home's original decoration. Throughout are examples of the 1950s furniture—which the owner and her friends are constantly hunting—that are beloved by today's Havana

hipsters. A Sputnik chandelier, heir to the crystal fixtures popular throughout Havana's history, floats over the sculptural wood base of a striking mid-century dining table.

Everything is kept deliberately simple—a quality of restraint that is rare in Havana's homes today. Muted fabrics and creamy leather upholstery allow the volumes to flow, connecting to views of the luxuriant garden out the glass walls found throughout. The home is all about light, space, and privacy. It is an expression of authentic Cuban style, albeit one strictly edited—an unusual exercise of discipline in this unabashedly eclectic city.

PREVIOUS PAGE

In a bedroom corridor, a mid-century-style swag-leg desk from Design Within Reach is paired with a vintage Cuban side chair and Venetian Baroque–style mirror.

BELOW

The whimsy of a painted iron garden chair brought indoors plays off a mid-century sofa upholstered in cream leather.

OPPOSITE

The seating areas of the living room appear to float in the soft light, with garden flowers and Murano glass decorations providing subtle pops of color.

6

Holding on to the Vanishing Past

Some of Havana's most interesting homes are especially representative of a specific neighborhood or of a particular moment in the city's architectural and cultural history.

These survivors of a Havana "frozen in time" make a direct connection to the city's Pre-Revolution glamour—especially the mid-century houses that bring to life the bustle of upper-middle-class neighborhoods developed during Havana's post–World War II prosperity.

The owners of these survivors of Havana's vanished past often speak of their role as caretakers of an aesthetic legacy, a responsibility they take quite seriously. From international-art books one might assume the city is packed with these time capsules, but they are increasingly becoming rare. These fast-disappearing remnants from another world evoke those bygone eras, only not with their dilapidation or romantic decay but with their aesthetic coherence. Since the Revolution, members of Havana's upper class who remained in their family homes often survived economic hardship by periodically selling pieces of colonial furniture or paintings by Cuban masters of the nineteenth and twentieth centuries. Consequently, only a handful of intact homes like Mary McCarthy's survive in Havana before their contents are also sold off and disbursed.

Many of Havana's Tropical Modernist houses of the 1950s conserve their original furnishings and fittings—excellent mid-century pieces imported as well as locally designed. These intimately scaled houses bear witness to the excellence of Cuban builders, architects, and decorators, and the sophistication of middle-class architectural patronage. They represent the search for national identity in architecture that successfully integrated centuries of Cuban home-building traditions with the International Style modernism popular at the time. These homes were conceived for the Cuban climate with a seamless integration of indoors and outdoors that is as prized today as it was in the 1950s.

That creative moment—associated with the construction boom of international hotels and casinos—was interrupted by the Cuban Revolution, which channeled talent and creativity away from the construction of single-family homes to projects that benefited a larger segment of the population: schools, hospitals, factories, and public housing. Today's designers can learn much from the houses completed just before this shift in priorities. Their scale, details, materials, and unmistakably Cuban essence are an inspiration for contemporary creators seeking to keep these rich aesthetic traditions relevant and alive.

The Mid-Century Search for a National Identity in Architecture
The Tropical Modern Homes of Havana

In 1960, Cuban master architect Eugenio Batista published an article in *Artes Plasticas* in praise of Frank Martinez's house for Eloisa Lezama Lima, completed the previous year. Batista celebrated the ambiguity he encountered in the house—which recalled Havana's colonial homes where the boundaries between interior and exterior spaces were often blurred. The author asks, Where exactly does the courtyard stop and where do the adjacent gallery spaces begin? In Martinez's work, as in the island's historic houses, courtyards became living rooms and galleries became more than just circulation spaces. This approach is one hallmark of the mid-century search for national identity in architecture (as well as in the arts). Batista urged the island's architects to embark on a comprehensive study of Cuba's architectural legacy in order to create houses that were essentially Cuban while being part of the contemporary world.

Batista's essay included several photographs of the sophisticated décor of the Lezama Lima house created by Clara Porset, which mixed Scandinavian pieces, updated versions of Cuban planter's chairs, geometric tile floors, and colored glass. Plants and wood louvers were everywhere, tile floors continued indoors and out, blurring the boundaries between interior and exterior—a logical way to live in the island's tropical climate.

Eugenio Batista and Frank Martinez were part of Havana's vibrant mid-century architecture scene that also included Rafael de Cardenas, Max Borges, Mario Romañach, Nicolas Quintana, and Emilio del Junco. Today in Havana, a handful of mid-century houses survive intact—preserving the integration of high-quality architecture with the original 1950s artwork and furnishings that were part of the architects' and owners' vision. Usually, a continuity of family ownership has preserved the architecture and the original decoration selected by the builders. Havana's contemporary designers could learn from the esthetic coherence found in these survivors of the city's design heyday. Already, some homeowners have fashioned their own interpretation of what a Pre-Revolution home would feel like, with its marriage of period architecture and appropriate furnishings—complete fabrications that successfully evoke the mood of a Havana home that might have been.

House of Eloisa Lezama Lima

Throughout the Eloísa Lezama Lima house, restrained compositions of operable louvers, colored glass, wood railings, and clay tile grilles were employed by architect Frank Martínez to provide a sense of scale and interest.

PREVIOUS PAGE, LEFT
The stair of the Pérez Farfante house, a mid-century gem by Frank Martínez, seems to float over the surrounding landscape.

PREVIOUS PAGE, TOP RIGHT
The pass-through of the Pérez Farfante kitchen was a design innovation reflecting a more informal lifestyle of the 1950s.

PREVIOUS PAGE, BOTTOM RIGHT
The neoclassical-style Cuban rocker is reminiscent of the original decoration of the Lezama Lima house.

House of Paulino Ingelmo

The 1951 Paulino Ingelmo house is an architectural icon in Nuevo Vedado—a three-story composition of concrete slabs and columns, an interpretation of the colonnades of Havana's neoclassical houses by architect Manuel Gutierrez.

A Mid-Century Villa in Lawton

The distinctive folding planes of the roof extend
beyond the mass of this house, shading a front balcony
and emphasizing the entry of the house below.

A Vedado Penthouse

The décor of this apartment is an interpretation of
a Pre-Revolution home created by a pair of self-taught
connoisseurs, successfully evoking the mood of
a Havana that might have been.

A Rare Survivor and the Custodian of Her Legacy

Mary McCarthy

Canadian-born Mary McCarthy was a Havana legend until her recent death at the age of 108. She became a member of the city's high society following her 1924 marriage to a Spanish-born Havana businessman. Mary taught piano and was a founding member of the Havana Philharmonic Orchestra. When her husband died in 1951, Mary took over the management of their leather goods factory, which had made great profits during World War II.

But Mary is best known for her life after the triumph of the Cuban Revolution. While all her society friends left in exile, Mary stayed put in her Country Club villa—even after the state seized her factory and other property. Mary's life became progressively more difficult as the US government blocked access to the fortune she had kept in Canadian banks. She was eventually granted a small monthly stipend after international newspapers reported on her constrained circumstances. Today, Mary's home is occupied by her heir, a Cuban said to have been among the many young boys aided in the Ciudad de los Niños, the Havana orphanage Mary founded. A talented pianist and a larger-than-life figure

himself, he venerates Mary and the home she left behind when she died.

Villa Mary is furnished today just as she left it, providing a unique opportunity to visit a survivor of Pre-Revolution Havana that is truly frozen in time. The antique-style furniture that was de rigueur in Havana's mansions is all here—all the Louis, Empire, Cuban colonial, and Spanish Renaissance style pieces. The decoration illustrates the eclectic taste that has been a Havana signature since the eighteenth and nineteenth centuries, when all manner of international pieces made their way to the city's docks and warehouses.

Unlike other homes of this genre, with their peeling plaster and dilapidated upholstery, everything at Villa Mary is well cared for, maintained as if it were a shrine. The house and its contents tell the story of the class that built Havana's elite residential neighborhoods and give insight into the sophisticated lifestyle they enjoyed. Mary is buried beside a marble sculpture in the extensive garden, which is a bit of the Cuba she never wanted to leave.

PREVIOUS PAGE

The central salon is presided over by a portrait of
Mary McCarthy in a black evening gown and with
Spanish fan. It is surrounded by the rugs, curtains,
and Louis XVI–style furniture she selected for her
Country Club home.

Swagged draperies remain at the headboard and
windows of Mary's former bedroom, which connects
to a Nile green dressing room decorated in the French
Empire style.

———

BELOW
Ornately carved mahogany cabinets define the dining
room, with Spanish Renaissance–style chairs at the
table as it is set for breakfast every morning.

A House Representing its Community
Ayleen Robainas

This mid-century, Tropical Modernist house might appear to be an unexpected choice for architect Ayleen Robaina, a specialist in eighteenth- and nineteenth-century architecture who has been a leading figure in Havana's historic preservation and planning agencies for decades. Yet, Ayleen has known the house all her life, having grown up nearby and attended school next door. In the 1970s, the woman who had built the house before the Revolution offered to swap it with the Robaina family's smaller home nearby. At the time, the exchange, or permuta, of houses was the only legal way for families to relocate in Cuba.

The 1958 house by Jaime Canaves is aesthetically in sync with its Nuevo Vedado neighborhood, which epitomizes the historical moment when the surrounding community was made up of Havana's professional class sharing the same aspirations as they built family houses. Ayleen's street preserves interesting examples of a variety of mid-century design directions, from the Cuban-inflected regional modernism of her own home to showy examples inspired by the Miami Beach style of the 1950s.

At the heart of the house is the terrace sitting room, where traditional rocking chairs enjoy views of a lush side courtyard. Rain or shine this is kind of space to gather—a source of light and air at the heart of the Cuban family home since the eighteenth century. Half a level below the terrace is the TV room, which is connected to the courtyard via louvered walls that frame the vistas as well as keep the air flowing. Up half a level from the terrace is the original master bedroom suite, occupied today by Ayleen's mother.

Working with a limited design palette of louvers framing views, the designer has achieved a kind of transparency that is the theme of the house. This is referenced by the living room's walls of adjustable louvers and the caning that keeps the curvaceous colonial seating furniture feeling cool in the tropical climate. The near emptiness of this and other rooms seems to celebrate the interior architecture, setting the mood for an abstracted modern aesthetic one of the possible "looks" of authentic Havana style to come.

PREVIOUS PAGE

The master bedroom is a box of louvers and glass surrounded by tropical vegetation—a modernist country cabin where an elaborate wirework sculpture serves as a headboard.

BELOW

At the core of this mid-century house is a covered outdoor space that acts as the central patio of the historic Cuban home—its walls of adjustable wood louvers keep the air flowing.

—

OPPOSITE

The visitor first encounters the formal salon, with its sinuous Cuban colonial furniture and collection of subtle works on paper by island masters.

Appropriating the Aesthetic of Decay

Pamela Ruiz & Damían Aquiles

Day or night, Pamela Ruiz and Damían Aquiles's house is buzzing with Damían's studio assistants working on projects, furniture restorers making a delivery, or cooks in the kitchen getting ready for an evening event. This Vedado home is a significant spot in Havana's cultural life, a gathering place where the international art world meets Cuban writers, photographers, musicians, and painters. The New York City–born Pamela takes her role as a cultural bridge very seriously. She's a confident hostess, carefully playing elements off each other—an approach she extends to the restoration and decoration of her family's unique home.

The house is at its romantic best at night. First-time guests arriving at the slightly mysterious site are unprepared for what follows—one of the most stylish and personality-filled homes in the city. Pamela's décor appropriates the aesthetic of decay that many associate with Havana and plays it off contemporary art, lacquered 1950s furniture, sparkling glass decorations, and dramatic lighting—making things feel anything but tired and run-down.

Damían is a talented artist whose creations are showcased throughout the house: his patchworks of painted metal or colorful action paintings are installed on top of the distressed wall paint or over panels of the original flowered wall paper that remain in the teal-painted salon.

A bar is set up on a glass table of the largest room, with a buffet dinner laid out on the mid-century table of the dining room. Guests lounge on upholstered banquettes in the garden, enjoying mojitos and Pamela's signature paellas.

This family home performs a dual professional role—as both a gallery for Damían's work and a site for cultural diplomacy where two worlds connect.

The homes of creative individuals illustrate their personal narratives, while preserving the story of the city around them. Homeowners like Pamela see themselves as caretakers of an aesthetic legacy, their furnishings and decorations injecting new life into a historic shell. This house effortlessly pairs the cliché of the decaying Pre-Revolutionary past with the vibrant life of today's Havana.

PAGE 144

A painting by Damían Aquiles presides over the dining room. Chandeliers are a Havana signature and here a 1950s fixture is an update of the more traditional hanging lights seen elsewhere in the city.

———

PREVIOUS PAGE

Wood posts support the front porch, a transitional area between the interior and the enveloping landscape. A globe sculpture by Aquiles provides visual interest and scale.

BELOW LEFT

The kitchen has been updated enough to function efficiently while remaining true to the spirit of the house.

———

BELOW RIGHT

Pieces come and go—currently a collection of Damían's metal spheres is a poetic installation in a corner of the dining room.

OPPOSITE

A corner of the living room shows where the original wallpaper was exposed above the painted wainscot. Vintage furniture and a turn-of-the-century light fixture contribute to the authentically Cuban aesthetic.

7

Personal Expression and Do-It-Yourself Decorating

Self-expression is at the heart of Havana's most interesting homes—which have long been havens of safety and comfort where owners can be their authentic selves. Unlike much home decorating in the "First World," none of these places was created from scratch at a single moment in time.

Consequently, these interiors are always evolving as owners are constantly on the hunt for just the right pieces. Havana's design aficionados love visiting other people's houses, remembering their special details and then incorporating these inspirations into their own homes. Pictures of their most recent vintage finds are constantly being shared on cell phones to ask for friends' opinions.

Havana's do-it-yourself decorators superimpose their design visions on their respective architectural contexts—seeing only what is beautiful and simply ignoring whatever might not fit their schemes. They create immersive environments—sanctuaries where they can disconnect from the island's harsh realities surrounded by their personal version of beauty. In their quest, they're constantly repurposing, recycling, and reimagining.

Family members—past and present—are important influences, with today's generation asserting their personal style while sharing the home with parents or living surrounded by family furniture. Their own possessions evoke their individual histories and experiences, artfully arranged so the house becomes something of a personal scrapbook. These homeowners get pleasure from the history of their city and celebrate their home's connection to the narrative of their surrounding community.

Havana Home Style Today

Encountering a stylish home on a side street of working class Centro Habana is a something of a surprise. Photographer Eduardo Hernandez has lived in his small apartment since before the Revolution, when his father owned the bodega downstairs. The family remained in their home after the state seized private businesses. What Eduardo's home lacks in size, it makes up for in personality, especially with his conviction to see only what is beautiful in the run-down surroundings, focusing on the dramatic vistas he's created within the home, employing glamorous touches like the orchid beautifully mixed with the huge tropical leaves. He shares this determination to focus only on the beautiful with the owners of other personality-filled Havana houses.

Many stylish Cubans are living in the homes their parents left them or sharing the places where they grew up in with their aging parents, the traditional extended family living as a reaction to the city's housing shortage. While many travel internationally, they are always drawn back to the touchstone of the family home, which they have personalized, surrounded by the family's furniture, legacy, and memories.

LEFT
Bamboo roller shades provide privacy and temper the sun in the intimacy of this garden porch in the Santos Suarez neighborhood.

TOP RIGHT
Modernist stools and interior architectural details in the bar of a mid-century Nuevo Vedado home.

BOTTOM RIGHT
Celita R. de Cardenas freshened up the interiors of the home her family built before the Revolution, recycling pieces that had been first installed by her grandmother in the 1950s.

The Home as a Treasure Cave

The owner of this 1950s apartment in Miramar is the descendant of one of the city's founding families. The photo albums he put together in the 1960s and 1970s record a diminishing number of upper-class friends gathering in this apartment, which became a meeting place for the bourgeois families that remained after the Revolution. Every time one of these friends departed, they left behind some keepsake in his care, some object that was critical to the telling of their own personal story. By default the owner of this apartment became an important, if unknown, custodian of Havana's past— of a bygone lifestyle represented by each of the objects that fills the apartment today.

The walls of the dining room are hung with dozens of dinner plates commissioned by Havana's ruling clans. This display is a centuries' old practice, which proclaimed a family's connection to the many coats of arms decorating those porcelain services. Elsewhere in the city, these plates would be mere wall decoration, but here each represents a departed family that was associated with his own at some moment in Havana's history, a souvenir of the vanished life enjoyed by the upper class before the 1959 Revolution.

Although he travels abroad to visit family, the owner of this apartment always returns—to his city, his treasure cave, to his beloved dog. He can't imagine abandoning his responsibility to the preservation of all these pieces that he venerates and that make life so rich and personal for him.

ABOVE

A nineteenth-century neoclassical sculpture is a focal point of the leafy terrace where Cuban colonial planter's chairs are a comfortable spot to enjoy the breeze.

OPPOSITE

German porcelain, Italian majolica and faience, bronze sculptures, European crystal, and a collection of porcelain dinner plates are among the apartment's treasures.

Pablo Armando Fernandez

The Miramar home of poet and novelist Pablo Armando Fernandez presents a conservative exterior that conceals an exuberant, private world. The recipient of Cuba's 1996 National Literary Award spent years living in New York before returning to Cuba at the time of the Revolution. Since then, he has lived in this Mediterranean Revival–style house, whose stone block walls are capped by ornate cornices holding up the clay tile roofs. The twisting shafts of Corinthian columns support arcades that define a shaded front porch set back behind a front garden.

Nothing prepares the visitor for the dynamic arches that define interior spaces while keeping the ground floor open. Areas flow into each other, as do the dramatic colored tiled floors. Hanging on the walls that occur between these arches is a significant collection of contemporary art that includes renown Cuban creators like Roberto Fabelo, Manuel Mendive and Wifredo Lam. In addition to portraits of Fernandez,

there are paintings and works on paper from the many places he has visited and participated in literary events—reminders of his connection to important international figures.

ABOVE

A series of dynamic arches define the spaces of this 1930s living room in Miramar, which is a traditional Mediterranean-style house on the outside.

156

Heriberto Cabezas

The owner of the top floor apartment of a 1950s duplex in Santos Suarez is a cosmopolitan man in charge of public relations at Ballet Nacional de Cuba. For years Heriberto Cabezas has worked with Alicia Alonso, organizing tours and performances at venues like the Paris Opera.

This intimately scaled home is another of Havana's cultural salons, where a unique mix of young artists, dancers, and film types overlap with sophisticated visitors and international Cubans of all generations.

Cabezas is one of a pack of Havana design groupies always on the lookout for curios and the vintage 1950s furniture he has been editing and upgrading. Throughout the apartment are contemporary Cuban paintings he has bought from artist friends. In spite of all his traveling, the apartment feels 100 percent Cuban—representative of this lively moment in design while perfectly suited to the 1950s setting.

ABOVE

A canvas by Adonis Ferro brings drama to the mid-century dining table and chairs, which complement the 1950s sideboard displaying Art Deco sculpture.

Juan Carlos Martinez & Michael Baez

Following years in their charming Old Havana home (page 108), this couple recently left behind the activity of the inner city for the more genteel Vedado—following the trajectory of Havana's middle-class families made more than a century ago. This move bears witness to a certain new mobility made possible by the recent reforms allowing the sale and purchase of real estate. Prior to this, the cumbersome *permuta*, or property exchange, was the only way a Cuban family could relocate—a process that could take years to complete.

Life in their Old Havana home had been centered on the interior courtyard, the traditional source of light and air for colonial houses. Now a glassed-in porch faces the front garden, set back from the street and filled with fanciful antique wicker seating and performs a similar function. The spaces of the previous apartment were interconnected in a traditional colonial style that kept the air flowing between rooms. In the Vedado

home, discrete spaces serve individual functions, as was popular in the early decades of the twentieth century. While much of their furniture has effortlessly become part of the house, one assumes the decoration of their new home will be a work in progress—and that these inventive design buffs would not have it any other way.

ABOVE LEFT
The kitchen is both elegant and unpretentious with caned French chairs, porcelains, an antique chandelier, and a plaster bust of a Cuban patriot.

ABOVE RIGHT
The garden gate is in keeping with the classical-style architecture popularized in turn-of-the-century Vedado.

OPPOSITE
A canopied bed made up with a toile de Jouy gives the guest bedroom an Old World ambience, as do the claw-foot stool, caned side chair and antique art work.

Art Tourism and a Cuban Family

Sandra Ramos

How does an artist establish personal privacy at home when dealing with busloads of international visitors who come to view her artwork? How can she balance the time spent chatting up these foreign clients—an investment that helps to sell the work—with the time required to actually produce the art? Artist Sandra Ramos lives and works in a 1920s house in the Kohly neighborhood, where her inviting front porch, set back in the garden and shaded by flowering shrubs, belies the professional nature of the home she shares with her parents and young daughter. The entire family is active in supporting the artist in an enterprise that provides for them all. There is a sense of organization to life here as they juggle appointments and keep things well supplied.

Room use has been kept in the traditional manner, beginning with the *saleta*, or formal parlor, and leading to the more comfortable family sitting area with the dining room at the rear of the house. Tall arches frame the transitions between these interconnected spaces, allowing the air to flow. These ground-floor rooms function as exhibition space, with Sandra's artwork hung on the walls, while maquettes and installation pieces are displayed throughout. The staircase is lit by a stained-glass window, designed by the artist, depicting a vulnerable female form.

Sandra is known internationally for her "Alice in Wonderland" imagery as well as for her fanciful maps of the island. She began her career during the hardships of the Special Period of the 1990s, and her art continues to reference Cuba's isolation and the sense of loss of the family members who have abandoned the island.

Sandra works in a variety of mediums—collage, painting, model making, and digital animation—in the modern studio she has built at the rear of the property. This new space allows her to spread out and pursue several ideas at once, while keeping the messier side of art-making outside of the family's home.

161

PREVIOUS PAGE

The geometries of the ornately carved front door recall elements from Sandra Ramos's works on paper displayed in the artist's entry vestibule.

———————

BELOW

The classical-style details of the early-twentieth-century front porch mingle with the tropical landscape in a quiet side street of the Kohly neighborhood.

OPPOSITE

The second-floor bedrooms and baths are charming—especially the master bedroom's suite of Renaissance Revival furniture given levity with boldly colorful accents.

162

High-Rise Living in Vedado

This stylish Vedado apartment tower is a reminder of the 1950s building boom that accompanied a surge in post–World War II tourism in Havana. The well-designed structure—with generous balconies and a dramatic interior stair—was built just blocks from the shops, movie theaters, and international hotels that made La Rampa the commercial hub of Havana on the eve of the Revolution. The apartment is the retreat of a single man who shares a traditional house with his extended family in a bustling Havana neighborhood, but who uses this getaway to entertain friends or to just hang out and watch movies.

The owner is a collector of Cuban contemporary art and a patron of emerging artists whom he helps by funding scholarships and competition prizes. This apartment affords him another set of walls on which to hang art—boldly scaled photographs and paintings, many of them portraits. While the paintings displayed in his family home tend toward Cuba's twentieth-century masters, the works in this apartment are younger and more provocative.

This art collection works well with the vintage Cuban-made furniture—mostly mid-century modern with some upholstered pieces in the Louis XV and Empire styles. These complement the interior architecture of flowing 1950s spaces, suggesting a tightly curated ensemble.

The glassed-in balcony is filled with sunlight during the day, while in the evening it enjoys an endless view of Havana's lights swept periodically by the lighthouse at the harbor's entrance. The apartment—floating above the bustle of the city—emanates a sense of well-being, and its detachment from Havana's noise and activity makes it the perfect getaway for someone so active in the city's social and culture scene.

PREVIOUS PAGE
A bold photograph by Jorge Otero hangs over
a mid-century sofa upholstered in natural canvas.
One of Havana's beloved glass-topped tables is
in the foreground.

———

BELOW
To the left of the dining table is a photorealist work by
Jorge Dager; over the table is a drawing by Arlés del Rio.

BELOW LEFT

In the 1950s this part of the Vedado experienced a construction boom, that was fueled by new zoning laws permitting taller structures like this building.

———

BELOW RIGHT

A painting of beach boys by Niels Reyes brings Cuba's waterfront lifestyle into a corner of this sophisticated, urban living room.

Entering an Immersive Environment
Ismael de la Caridad

The oceanfront apartment of fashion designer Ismael de la Caridad provokes a strong emotional response from the visitor entering his private world for the first time—an unexpected Victorian extravaganza transported to a 1950s tower overlooking the Malecón. Ismael has managed to create a cozy, mysterious ambiance while surrounded by the bright Cuban light and overlooking the endless sea. Most people would have focused the interior design on the spectacular view, but instead he chose to turn inward. Ismael's home is about the fantasy of taking a high-rise apartment of the kind found anywhere in the world and creating his own theatrical vision of bygone Havana.

Ismael has taken the open-plan floor of 1950s construction and superimposed his own aesthetic, adding a sense of perspective and framed vistas and the feeling of traditional, individual rooms. Salvaged columns "support" the apartment's structural beams, which have been decorated with painted stencils, while doorways have been cased with antique mahogany frames and provided with salvaged stained-glass doors.

Havana's beloved crystal chandeliers have been reconfigured, compressed so they fit within the lower ceilings of the 1950s space—an outlandish yet effective solution. Antique cut glass shimmers everywhere in the light, contrasting with intense wall colors like terracotta, turquoise, and navy blue. Havana's colonial furniture is often seen in sad, dusty settings as dark and lifeless pieces a family has used for generations. Ismael takes these constants of Havana style—nineteenth-century furniture, stained glass, crystal chandeliers, and the abundance of "stuff"—and employs them in incongruous juxtapositions that make these pieces come alive. His Havana style is creative without getting bogged down by the practicalities that are at the core of the daily grind for most of those living on the island.

Ismael claims he can completely transform the apartment overnight, switching out the contents and presenting an entirely new narrative in his home—one just as uninhibited, no doubt, another private vision that has been waiting in the wings for the opportunity to make itself felt, a world that will be just as convincing.

PAGE 168
The vivid colors of Zaida del Rio's painting of the Virgin Mary provide a sense of architecture above prized Cuban pieces including an eighteenth-century sacristy chest and a nineteenth-century caned armchair.

———

PREVIOUS PAGE
Cut-glass decorations sparkle on the glass-topped dining table, while at the windows folding *mamparas* and salvaged stained-glass panels seem to intensify the Cuban light.

BELOW
Ismael has created one of Havana's most inventive kitchens, an extension of the apartment's open plan, connected aesthetically by the emerald-green wall color that sets off the antique mahogany cabinetry.

OPPOSITE
The master bedroom is a courtesan's dream: tassels, fringe, brocades, and a mirrored ceiling are softly lit by a pair of bronze ladies while polychrome angels guard the foot of the ornate Victorian bedstead.

8

Havana's Homegrown New Guard

Havana's homegrown elite includes the Cuban executives of international firms operating in Havana as well as the city's foreign residents, all of whom are deeply committed to their city.

Their lifestyle presents an idea of Havana style to come—a vision of the future that is firmly rooted in the city's traditions. Much of this New Guard prefers an authentic Havana aesthetic and is uninterested in a retread of Miami Beach glitzy glamour. As the city's fledgling real-estate market grows, properties are changing hands and home renovations are beginning to make an impact on parts of the city—especially in its historic core.

Members of Havana's New Guard take seriously their role as custodians of the historic houses they feel fortunate to inhabit. They understand how the architecture and interior details of their homes connect to specific moments in Havana's past. In these homes, staff members care for gardens and interiors while the homeowners are constantly upgrading artwork and furnishings to ensure they are stylistically appropriate to the distinctive architecture.

In today's Havana, there has been a rediscovery of hospitality, which connects to the graciousness of life in the city prior to the privations of the Special Period of the 1990s.

Havana of the future will also rely on the participation of Cubans currently living abroad, who have never stopped loving their island and who will return to Havana to contribute to the making of their city's future while remaining connected to the outside world.

The Glamour of Havana to Come

Rachel Valdés Camejo

Talented Havana artist Rachel Valdés Camejo and her Catalan husband personify Havana's New Guard of today—Cuban art world meeting European business world, with an international sophistication that is grounded in a love of Cuban culture. Their home is an example of the best of Havana's Old Guard architecture—a 1930s, Spanish Colonial house designed for Javier del Valle, one of a quartet of famously wealthy brothers. The large property remains unchanged on a very private cul-de-sac in the exclusive Country Club district. Clusters of magnificent royal palms shade the swimming pool, defining areas in the garden, which is a perfect venue for memorable parties.

When a photo of Rachel graced the cover of Michael Dweck's book *Habana Libre*, published in 2011, she instantly became the face of Havana privilege previously unknown to the outside world. Rachel and her sophisticated home epitomize the future of Havana style. Her decorating centers on a confident mix of 1950s Cuban pieces, contemporary furniture brought from Europe, and her own large-scale paintings—all complementing the house's architectural details.

Although Rachel's décor features plenty of mid-century Cuban furniture, it never feels vintage but instead thoroughly of the moment. This is truly Havana style to come: an atmosphere that is Cuban, contemporary, and very much of the international world. Rachel is a modern incarnation of her national identity: proud of being descended from a long line of strong Cuban women who juggle marriage, a successful career, and motherhood. Rachel keeps the art-making out of the family home, working at a large studio space in Vedado. In the last years, her art has evolved from colorful, representational paintings to luminous, abstract pieces. A series of large-scale installations have been exhibited internationally to critical acclaim. Examples of works in each of these media are found throughout the house and its surrounding property—where they are paired with pieces by many of Cuba's hottest artists, making for an especially successful integration of historic architecture, contemporary art, and a comfortable lifestyle.

PAGE 176
The spacious and light-filled kitchen is dominated by the center island with its contemporary stools. Here too, mid-century furniture and contemporary Cuban art are casually displayed.

———

BELOW
A view of the living room, whose arched doors are architectural quotations from the original builder's ancestral home in provincial Trinidad.

PREVIOUS PAGE
Rachel Valdés Camejo's provocative artwork sets the mood for different areas of the house. This portrait of an Eastern European woman commands the living room; to its left hangs one of a pair of paintings by Roberto Diago.

OPPOSITE
The del Valle family coat of arms is centered on the side elevation of the Cuban colonial–style exterior of the house, which is nestled among the royal palms of the extensive property.

The Custodians of Havana's Past
Family Life in La Vibora

The owner of this neoclassical-style house is one of a growing number of Havana natives who maintain homes both in the Cuban capital and abroad. Running a successful Latin America–based business, he spends half his time in the Havana home he shares with several generations of his family. This house represents Havana style to come, as more and more Cubans who have created successful careers off the island are returning to their native city to enjoy its more leisurely pace, surrounded by family members and their memories. Politics aside, their investment in the city will help to awaken the sleeping beauty, revitalizing neighborhoods they know well.

The turn-of-the-century architecture of this house dates from a moment in time whose evidence is fast disappearing. Both the décor and the family's lifestyle is traditional—and feels almost unchanged since the early twentieth century, when the house was constructed. The house displays the classic layout of the period, when courtyards were no longer needed at the center of the freestanding house. Instead an American–style hall was at the heart of the home— a vertical volume defined by oversize decorative columns with shafts of colorful faux marble marking the entrances to formal spaces. This hall is lit and ventilated by skylights and operable transoms that bathe the interior of the house in light, which perfectly suits the tropical plants found growing everywhere. To right and left of this interior spine are the family's bedrooms and baths. Traditional Cuban details like the *mamparas*, Gothic-style, low doors of carved wood and glass, are used at the entrances to bedrooms to provide both ventilation and privacy.

The decoration of the house relies on Cuban favorites like nineteenth-century European porcelain, white painted American-made wicker furniture, and the owner's collection of Cuban art of the early twentieth century, which includes paintings by Servando Cabrera Moreno, Fidelio Ponce de León, and Jaime Valls and Mariano. The owner and his family see themselves as custodians of the historic architecture that they inhabit and, by extension, protectors of the community that surrounds them.

183

PREVIOUS PAGE

The front and sides of the house are wrapped in shaded porches, where today, as in the past, the family gathers to enjoy the breeze at different times of day.

———

BELOW

The top-lit center hall is a circulation space at the core of the house, defined at either end by colorful stucco columns. At the right is a 1930s painting by Fidelio Ponce de León.

OPPOSITE

The living room includes seating in the Louis XV style as well as Victorian, Art Nouveau, and Spanish Renaissance styles paired with oversize contemporary Cuban artwork.

Mid-Century Connoisseurship
Nora Belanzaurán & Otto Hermos

The owners of this mid-century home personify today's Havana hospitality—a balance of the love of entertaining with an appreciation and care for their historic house. They represent a homegrown New Guard grounded in Cuban traditions. While some of the city's graciousness has been lost since the Revolution and subsequent Special Period, the wife has been keeping alive the tradition of making guests feel welcome. She often defers to the recommendations of her aged housekeeper, once employed by Havana's French ambassadors, who recalls how things were done exactly *comme il faut* before the political upheavals.

The stylish wife is particularly proud of her mid-century house, designed by Havana master Frank Martínez in the elite Siboney neighborhood. One could say that caring for the structure has become her life's work. The house has all the hallmarks of Tropical Modernist homes of the 1950s, including the walls of adjustable louvers that fold away, connecting the interiors to the surrounding gardens and the courtyard at the building's core. It is exhilarating to witness this transformation of the interior of the home into a sequence of spaces that are neither solely indoors nor outdoors but something in-between.

The architect's deliberately simple palette of materials ensures the seamless integration of interior and exterior, framing vistas within the house or out to the tropical landscape. Interlocking volumes are lit by stained-glass clerestory windows that dapple the tropical sun while conveying an ideal of "Cuban-ness" that was popular with the Cuba's mid-century modernist architects. Havana designers are once again grappling with making design choices that say "Cuban"—once again incorporating references to the island's historic building traditions while being thoroughly of the modern world. The furnishings found in the house today bear witness to the sophistication of Havana's Pre-Revolution lifestyle—particularly the exuberant Hollywood Baroque dining table, an unexpected piece that is surrounded by the original dining chairs the wife snagged from their original setting.

OPENER

Wood louvered doors are folded back to open the rooms up to one another, as well as the interior to the gardens all around. Colored glass sidelights and clerestory windows temper the sunlight, recalling traditional Cuban architecture.

PREVIOUS PAGE

Paintings by Carlos Quintana face each other across the living room—a volume of its own with windows on three exposures—where the family's TV and computers are found.

OPPOSITE

The couple are known for their gracious hospitality: here the rear terrace is set for breakfast overlooking the palms and bamboos of the extensive garden.

——

BELOW

Nora found the dining room's 1950s Baroque-style table and en suite chairs in a house that had been decorated in the grand manner before the 1959 Revolution.

9

Havana Style
to Come

In the past year, home renovations in Havana have increased as a result of the newly permitted buying and selling of real estate. Many structures are being upgraded by new homeowners, while others are being repurposed as restaurants, bars, and guesthouses—microenterprises now allowed by the Cuban government.

Recently, Airbnb has put thousands of Havana homestays online, connecting American visitors for the first time to the way Cubans live. If the thaw in US-Cuba diplomatic relations continues, these newly sanctioned private initiatives will flourish and a positive economic impact should be visible in parts of the city. Elite homeowners are paying more attention to the service spaces of their homes, importing kitchen cabinets, fitted closet interiors, high-end appliances, and specialty plumbing fixtures from abroad.

Up till now, Havana homes were by necessity the product of renovations of pre-1960 architecture that often took place piecemeal over time. If changes continue, it will be liberating for homeowners to build their houses from the ground up if they are so inclined, no longer being constrained by working with existing structures. Demolitions of historic building will be inevitable and further protections of individual landmarks and historic neighborhoods will be urgently required. Many residents are expressing fears regarding aggressive or inappropriate development by foreign investors avid to get in on the "Cuban moment." However, this is outweighed by excitement and optimism about everything the future could bring.

Foreign-based Cubans will be among the first to completely reimagine the Havana home, fusing the best aspects of their international lifestyles with beloved Cuban traditions. Cuban artists and musicians living abroad are already establishing Havana bases of operation, effortlessly transporting their "downtown" lifestyle to the tropics.

Even the American Ambassador's Residence—the physical embodiment of the US presence in Havana—will inevitably reconnect to the city, reflecting the new communication that follows the misunderstandings of the past fifty years. The visiting American trade missions, academics, potential investors, congressional committees, and professional groups are a growing community that Havana's American diplomats will now need to serve.

It is only a matter of time before Americans are among the developers investing in Havana's future. One hopes they will recognize that discerning tourists respond to the authentic Cuban style found in these pages, which embodies the city's memories. In time, Havana's design narrative will incorporate elements that recall the years of revolution—and not just the art that comments on this recent past—but furniture and other pieces that reference decades of the ingenuity and repurposing that characterized the last fifty years.

Building for the Next Generation
Karem Pérez & Jorge Araoz

Karem Pérez and Jorge Araoz are as cosmopolitan as a Havana couple can get: intelligent, sophisticated, funny, and incredibly warm and welcoming. Their mid-century, suburban Havana house has been updated with contemporary appliances, lighting, plumbing fixtures, and kitchen cabinets. Their concern with aesthetics extends to the airy service areas—something unusual in Havana and a sign of their international exposure.

But today's light-filled spaces are only the core of a future house the couple dreams of building on this generous property. They hope to add two-story wings and open courtyards, defining interlocking spaces that will accommodate houseguests as well as their two Europe-based daughters, gathering the family together in the spirit of extended family living that has long been a Cuban trademark. A new pool, to be built between the proposed and the existing buildings, will anchor an extensive indoor-outdoor entertaining space—which has always been a hallmark of Havana's residential style. In a holdover from the attitudes of the recent past, the street front will be kept discreet and noncommittal, guarding the family's privacy from the outsider's gaze.

The couple's recent experience with Havana's new freelance designers has had its ups and downs. Until now, Cuban architects have never worked with private clients—so local designers have been frustrated for decades, gathering images of the many design ideas they hope to incorporate into their independent projects. But Karem was not interested in building a repertoire of someone else's design tricks. In yet another example of Cuban resourcefulness, she taught herself computer drafting so she could put down on paper exactly what she felt the project needed. She has recently been working directly with a builder to begin creating a home for future generations.

PREVIOUS PAGE

Four Harry Bertoia–style chairs gather around a 1950s cocktail table in one of the open-air courtyards that are a signature of the house.

BELOW

In the living room, sleek 1950s armchairs and footstools and a Cuban colonial pedestal table mix with upholstered furniture the couple imported from Latin America.

BELOW LEFT

Karem has chosen her mid-century furniture astutely: knockout pieces include the fantastic glass-topped dining table combined with gold-painted Louis XVI–style chairs, conveying a very international feeling.

BELOW RIGHT

Open-air support spaces are protected from sun and rain by a floating parasol roof. Low stone walls shelter an outdoor corridor that is shaded by climbing elephant ears and leafy banana trees.

Cucu Diamantes & Andres Levin

Singer Cucu Diamantes and music producer Andres Levin are a Havana power couple connected to the city's political and cultural elite, as well as creative types off the island. The New York–based, Grammy Award winners are constantly sponsoring collaborations with locals in the music and art world, including the first Havana TED Talk, which Andres hopes to repeat annually.

The renovation of their Miramar penthouse apartment is representative of today's Havana style, announcing the look of a Havana yet to come. Like the fusion music they create, their new home combines the best of the "outside" world with the best of the island. Their architects, Claudia Castillo and Orlando Inclán of the firm habana[re]generacíon, are considered experts in the revitalization of Havana's historic neighborhoods that many are convinced is about to take place. Without intending to, Cucu and Andres have transported to the tropics the artists' loft spaces they know well from their lives in downtown New York. Their home's open-plan living feels especially appropriate in Havana—for centuries, interconnecting rooms were a traditional and effective way of ensuring air flow in Cuba's colonial houses.

An open combination kitchen and dining area dominates the space while defining several seating areas and an office on the fringes. The concrete slab of the ceiling has been left exposed, providing a patina usually associated with Havana's moldering historic architecture, and is used here without any implications of decay. The original cream-colored terrazzo floors have been supplemented with areas of the colorful encaustic tiles so representative of traditional Havana décor. Playing with the historic shell is fairly new in Havana, leading to the question: how much can one intervene and still have the space feel original?

This new home represents the renovation fever hitting the city's elite, with owners anxious to imprint their personalities on newly purchased homes. The loft exhibits the first incarnations of a design approach that is sure to appear throughout the city: the play of delicate crystal chandeliers against rough concrete surfaces, the display of vintage kitchen appliances, the use of salvaged construction materials, and the focus on spacious, well-appointed dressing rooms and baths. Taken together, these elements herald the new Havana brand.

PAGE 198

A rustic wood vanity cabinet backs up to a low concrete partition in the open-plan master bathroom, where a claw-foot tub floats over a traditional Cuban tile floor.

———

BELOW

The grand piano is a de rigueur element in a musician's home. The 1920s rocking chair is a design variation of a beloved Cuban piece of furniture.

OPPOSITE

The award-winning Vibra chair by Raiko Valladares and José A. Villa is a new icon of contemporary Cuban design.

PREVIOUS PAGE

Wood louver windows on four exposures keep the loft bright and breezy. The poured concrete ceiling was left unpainted, while areas of traditional tile floor are surrounded by the penthouse apartment's original terrazzo floors.

Simple Places to Share with Friends

Before 1959, many affluent Cubans owned simple beach houses just outside the city or more elaborate getaways on the fabled Varadero beach. Following the Revolution, the state allowed Cubans to retain their vacation homes in addition to their primary residences. A small group of today's elite has recently been purchasing properties in several small beach towns outside Havana. The décor of these getaways is kept effortless, conveying the notion of escape from responsibilities and allowing a spontaneity of use as an extension of the owner's city entertaining.

Thirty minutes to the east of Havana, past large-scale housing projects synonymous with the Revolution is the low-key beach town of Guanabo, one of the Playas del Este that Havana residents turn to in the heat of summer. At the top of a hill overlooking Guanabo is the mid-century beach house recently renovated by a Havana entrepreneur, a producer of music events on the island and abroad. Nothing could be easier than driving out to the beach house to enjoy sunset cocktails and returning in time for dinner in Old Havana. Conversely, a night of clubbing is often capped by a sunrise breakfast served on the beach house's enormous roof terrace. Four bedrooms are always ready in case friends want to spend the night.

Half an hour west of Havana is the rural beach town of Banes, where architect Carlos Ferreira has designed a rustic getaway. Here, vegetables and herbs from the garden are always on the menu, especially for the impromptu lunches on Sunday afternoons. The décor hits just the right note, whether in the unpretentious kitchen, in the sitting room used during rainstorms, or on the oceanfront porch where guests spend most of their time.

LEFT
Blue walls and a green painted ceiling connect this Miramar sitting room to the swimming pool and ocean beyond.

TOP RIGHT
The living room of the Banes beach house is furnished as simply as possible—since visitors spend all their time outdoors.

BOTTOM RIGHT
The piano-shaped swimming pool of architect Miguel Gaston's waterfront home. The house, built in the 1950s, is today an elegant *paladar*, or home restaurant.

A Beach House in Guanabo

A 1950s sideboard is placed outside the combination
breakfast room and greenhouse of this Guanabo
beach house, with a painting by Jorge López Pardo and
Havana's beloved Murano decorations.

OPPOSITE
A contemporary painting by Alex Hernández Dueñas
perfectly captures the escapist mood of this Guanabo
beach house.

A Beach House in Guanabo

Views of the Straits of Florida from one of several
terraces overlooking the small beachfront town
of Guanabo.

A Rustic Getaway in Banes

The kitchen of the Banes beach house is simply
fitted out with hardwood cabinets made by
a local woodworker.

The American Ambassador's Residence

Ever since the resumption of diplomatic relations between Cuba and the United States culminating in President Barack Obama's visit in 2015, attention is being paid to America's top diplomat on the island and the home in which his family lives. Set on a quiet, jungly street in the elite Country Club district, this area is one of the most security-conscious places in Havana.

The American Ambassador's Residence was designed to be the most impressive US residence in the Western Hemisphere—a signal of Cuba's importance in the region. Before the Revolution, the residence hosted receptions for the island's American community and members of Havana's high society, as well as American and Cuban politicos. In the 1950s the American ambassador was known as the number-two man on the island.

The aesthetic language of the residence, with its golden Jaimanitas stone exterior, conveys a fortress-like solidity. Since the Revolution, its style of architecture and secluded grounds have emphasized a detachment from the life of the island. In the last two years, Ambassador Jeffrey DeLaurentis has been injecting personality into the residence's public spaces with artwork by American creators, often artists that he and his wife, Jennifer, have admired or collected. These bold new pieces playing off the historic architecture and traditional decoration add individuality and contemporary style. The State Department's Art in Embassies program and the Foundation for Art and Preservation in Embassies have provided works by a variety of US artists.

The residence's furniture looks as if it has been there a long time. (Keeping the décor looking fresh has been challenging because of the embargo.) Following decades of cosmetic maintenance, this grand, historic house will need to be updated to suit today's détente-friendly lifestyle.

After fifty years of isolation, the complicated symbolism of the residence will remain, acknowledging the years of estrangement in order to collaborate better as nations embarking on building a new future together. The current role of this emblematic house will expand and reflect an American openness as the grounds and interiors are redefined for modern times.

PREVIOUS PAGE

In the stair hall two appropriately themed pieces by Steve Miller—from the Art in Embassies project—contrast with the traditional furniture.

———

BELOW

One of a pair of japanned cabinets on giltwood stands that have been in the residence since the 1950s, with a pair of Sheraton-style shield-back chairs nearby.

OPPOSITE

A William Wegman photo hangs over the fireplace of the wood paneled library, imparting an extra coziness to the fireside setting.

FOLLOWING PAGES

The butterfly-shaped floor plan of the United States ambassador's residence ensures cross-ventilation, making the large house appear less massive as it cascades down into the surrounding landscape.

Osmani Hernández & Casa Vitrales

Casa Vitrales is a pioneering concept in Havana tourism—a successful example of private initiative in the city's historic core. Vitrales represents the future of Havana: the small, independent, highly personal, and stylish places for savvy visitors to sleep or dine. Already, Vitrales is functioning as a catalyst for a new phase of its historic neighborhood—a not yet prettified part of Old Havana—with two new restaurants recently opened nearby. This moment in Havana's design history is marked by clever entrepreneurs using design to distinguish their businesses from the competition.

Simple, good design appeals to Vitrales's sophisticated clientele—mostly Europeans—looking for a genuine "people to people" exchange that they cannot get in the larger tourist hotels and a feeling that they're in the know, connected to the real Havana. Yet, this is not the Airbnb experience—Vitrales provides service, albeit in a low-key way.

Vitrales was created by Osmani Hernández in a four-story, nineteenth-century building and is named for the colored-glass windows that are a hallmark of Cuba's historic architecture. Originally a single-family home above a ground-floor commercial space, the house was reconfigured to focus on getting light and air into its interior. Osmani and his family spend long days attending to guests, caring for the house, and responding to the constant challenges posed by Havana's decrepit infrastructure.

Osmani's warm personality and sense of humor mask his obsessive attention to detail. Time spent abroad makes him a host with the highest of standards, but he is also a sophisticated design consumer. Vitrales's public areas play Cuban design constants off each other—*mamparas*, or low screen doors, and colored glass, vivid floor tiles, 1950s furniture, contemporary art, and colonial pieces—in a way that is unmistakably Havana of today. One hopes the city's designers will see the value in this authentic Cuban style, which tourists will appreciate.

LEFT
The living room of Casa Vitrales introduces the visitor to the constants of Havana-style decorating: wood louvered doors, stained-glass transoms, colorful tile floors, mid-century furniture, and exuberant contemporary art.

BELOW LEFT

A mid-century breakfast table and chairs in the eat-in kitchen, with windows open to the bustle of the Old Havana setting beyond.

—————

BELOW RIGHT

A monochrome portrait of José Martí, the father of Cuban independence, overlooks a settee in the Vitrales living room.

OPPOSITE

Casa Vitrales's rooftop terrace is the perfect place to lounge in the sunshine or enjoy a sunset cocktail overlooking the Old Havana skyline.

Havana Tastemakers Today

Havana today is buzzing with the birth of a real-estate market and renovations related to the new microenterprises that are employing as many as 500,000 Cubans and helping to create a new middle-class. The best of these new shops and restaurants illustrate the power of design to give businesses a unique identity, as professionals make esthetic statements that acknowledge Cuba's design history.

Havana's historic architecture will be increasingly under pressure from Cuban as well as international developers, as thousands of hotel rooms are constructed in the historic city. The best visions for Havana's future will balance preservation with contemporary needs and be mindful of local communities.

Acknowledgments & Credits

This book could not have been created without the help of many people—both in Havana and abroad—over a period of several years. I received a warm welcome at every home I visited while producing *Havana Living Today*—a testament to the city's hospitality and the average Cuban's pride in their architectural patrimony. My gratitude to the special friends who ardently supported this project and took it to heart, making a point of seeking out stylish homes and interesting homeowners for me to visit. At the top of this list were Norwegian Ambassador John-Petter Opdahl and his husband Francisco A. Cabrera Gatell, who were supportive for years. Always enthusiastic were Moraima Clavijo Colom, Heriberto Cabezas, Karem Perez Espin, Virginia Morales Menocal, and Jose Camilo Valls. Swedish Ambassador Elisabeth Eklund shared her interest in Cuban architecture and offered me her own brand of Havana hospitality. Katharina Voss, Ella Cisneros, Cucu Diamantes, Alejandro Alonso, the late Pedro Contreras, and Pietro de Martin opened doors and shared their appreciation for authentic Havana style.

It was a privilege to be working on this project while US Ambassador Jeffrey DeLaurentis was serving in Havana. He and his wife, Jennifer, have done historic work for Cuba-US relations. They offered me their support and friendship as well as their special insight into issues related to the aesthetics.

LEFT

The outdoor spiral stair at Lab.26 is a colorful re-imagination of a traditional form.

PREVIOUS PAGE, TOP LEFT

The new rooftop bar at La Guardia, recently renovated by Habana Re-generation.

PREVIOUS PAGE, TOP RIGHT

331 Art Space is the most sophisticated of Havana's private galleries, displaying the works of Adrián Fernández, Alex Hernández Dueñas, and Frank Mujica Chavéz.

PREVIOUS PAGE, BOTTOM RIGHT

Working with what is at hand, the owners completely furnished this garage apartment, available on Airbnb, with shipping pallets.

PREVIOUS PAGE, BOTTOM LEFT

A contemporary-style stair floats in the center hall of La Reserva, Havana's most stylish new boutique hotel.

New York friends offering their expertise and special advice included Ramiro Fernandez, Rafael Diaz Casas and David Freeland, Iliana Cepero, Jasper Goldman, Jim Friedlander and Academic Arrangements Abroad. Chas A. Miller III was always supportive, as were the Friends of the Sir John Soane Museum.

Among the many friends in Havana making introductions were Reny Martinez, Siomara Sanchez Robert, Daniel Taboada, Margarita Alarcon, Carlos Ferreira, Eduardo Hernandez, Jose Antonio Choy and Julia de Leon, and Nivaldo Carbonnell. Gracious homeowners include Italian Ambassador Carmine Robustelli and Irene Burrigo, Spanish Ambassador Juan Francisco Montalban and Pilar Rubi, and Swiss Ambassador Anne Pascale Krauer-Mueller. Photographers Carlos Otero and Alain Gutierrez made beautiful contributions to this volume.

My partner, Carey Maloney, enthusiastically supported this project during every phase of its production. This book would not have been possible without his commitment and his sharing of my mission to bring all this Havana glamour into the light. My special thanks to photographer Adrián Fernández, who has worked with me from the beginning—together we have learned about his native Havana, documenting centuries of outstanding design.

This book is a celebration of the idea of home as a haven. I respectfully acknowledge the creativity and imagination of Cuban homeowners working with so little who have achieved dreams, in celebration of their love of beauty.

Photographs are by Adrián Fernández, unless otherwise specified below:

Alain L. Gutierrez: Pages 31, 86, 102 (right), 124, 126, 140, 142, 143, 202, 206, 208, 212
Carlos Otero: Pages 45, 62, 82, 84, 85, 92, 94, 95, 190, 198, 200–201, 204 (top right), 209

First published in the United States of America in 2017 by
Rizzoli International Publications, Inc.
300 Park Avenue South
New York, NY 10010
www.rizzoliusa.com

Designed by: MGMT. design

ISBN: 978-0-8478-5880-4
Library of Congress Control Number: 2017944939

Copyright 2017 Rizzoli International Publications
Text copyright 2017 Hermes Mallea

Printed in China

2017 2018 2019 2020 2021 / 10 9 8 7 6 5 4 3 2 1